The Search for Still Waters

Alan Creedon

Cover artwork: Lucy Barker https://lucy-barker.co.uk/
Cover design: Declan Durcan
ISBN: 978-1-7399578-8-9

BOOKHUB©

PUBLISHING

Published by Book Hub Publishing, An Independent Publishing House with Offices in Galway and Limerick, Ireland.
www.bookhubpublishing.com
@BookHubPublish @ThesisClinic

Book Hub Publishing is committed to inclusion and diversity. We print our books on forestry sustainable paper.

Dedication

For Eilish, Ted, Sooze, Aoife, Siún, Beth, Rae
and Cosmo.

Acknowledgements

So many people to thank and send masses of gratitude to, those who helped with the walk, lent me kit, supported and inspired me, taught me stuff, put me up, put me in my place, lent me their music, everything leading up to and including the walk, in no particular order at all:

Explorers Connect, Ged, Bev and the boys, The Mudhutters Farm and the Harrisons, James Golden, Rachel, Bryn, Twm, Sydna, Gwil, Ann, Carl, Joe Pollitt, Jo, The fella in the hotel, The Vis family, Sam and David for playing for free, Rioghnach and Ellis for playing for free, everyone who could see that I was what I was doing came from my heart, DBH Dan for playing for free, Alix Walker, Paddy Steer, All the Amazing Staff at Superkids in Levenshulme, All FM, Mike Alexander for supporting me and taking me across the sea without really even knowing me, Anglesey Outdoors, Séamus and Steph, Paddy and Anne McMahon, Dee McMahon, Nora and Paddy in Clondalkin, Anne and Maria in Sallins, Rita, Arthur and family, Alistair Humphreys, Gene Courtney, Uncle Jim, Uncle Tom, Paula Sheehy-Gilarde, My American Family – too many to name! My Irish uncles and aunts, Natalie, Joe and the boys, people who told me I would not make it across the Irish Sea in a kayak, Colin Shanahan, Eddy Ashworth, Helen Kelly, Manchester Mind, Camphill Dingle, Tom Doolin, Joe the Baker and all at Cloughjordan Ecovillage, Susan Wray and the Nenagh family, Father John in Birdhill, Fr David in Birr, Eimear the physio, staff at Nenagh hospital, Mag and Tom Shanley and family, Lisa Lorenz, Lee Jones, Nuala Moore for advising me about supplements in my depleted state, Ferg Flannery for the free website and design (thanks!), Jay Gearing for the free promo vids, Triona Duignan for gig organizing and fundraising, Al and Erika for the surprise visit, Harry Needs for the free (and sometimes torturous) PT plan, Martin Logan and all at Irish TV, The gang at Unicorn including Gabor Parlag, Dan Weston and others who lent me gear, Greg and Susie, Sarah, Trish, Peter, Adam and Charlotte at Glebelands for putting up with me and helping me have a great experience, Amrita Mamasita, Jana Hendrickson, Marian O Flaherty, Nick, Adele, Isaac and Otis, people who opened their hearts to me on the walk, The guy with the drone at Porth Dafarch, the guy on the bike, everyone who questioned why I would want to paddle across the Irish Sea, the people who shared stories, those who listened, Tommy, Tina and family, the, Fitzgerald's of Dingle, the lady in Castlegregory who put us up in the B&B for free and whose name I can't find, Seán Mac an tSithigh, and of course the hundreds of generous people who donated to raise almost £10k for Manchester Mind and over €14k for Camphill Dingle and everyone who had a sponsorship form in their premises in and around Dingle.

Thanks to Niall and all at Book Hub Publishing and Lucy for the cover design.

Opening

Walking up the track I see the golden light ahead and brace myself for its rays to reach my face. It's autumn and as the bracken's summer greens fade to yellow, then rusty brown, the bright sunlight catches them, bringing them to life again and they glow like flames, as if to give off one more blast of light before they give way to decay. I can't get enough of this light. These past two weeks have shown me more intense beauty than I noticed the whole summer past, immersed in greenness.

Heading up the fields I scan the ground for mushrooms, walking into the wind's resistance. I zip up my jacket, grateful that I put it on as when I left home it didn't seem that windy or cold and I almost didn't bring it. I search out spots in the hills where I can sit, where I can have a view and sit. But today I'm restless, seeking something, and the blurred ruin of an old stone farmhouse with no apparent track to it, shows me lives that have been and faded away, above the sound of freight trains on the valley bottom. The whump, whump of the wind turbines capture the regular, reliable wind supply as it hits the western Pennines from the flat western plains towards the Irish Sea.

Today I want to go somewhere different, to experience a new place – that's what I do when I feel a bit stuck. I find a new path down the side of a steep, hummocky moorland hill, watching my steps as I go, eyeing up places to stop and sit. I want to check out a fenced off plantation so I follow the line of the fence down steep, lumpy grassy sides, squelching through boggy patches between the half ruined stone wall and the sheep wire fence. I see a bird take off below me, sure of flight and direction. It's a bird of prey with speckled, lichenous wings – maybe a little owl. I find a gap in the fence – more a gash than a gap. The entire fence cut through and pulled aside was a surprise to find. Perhaps the farmer had decided it was time to let the sheep in. The feeling in amongst the trees is different to the open, windy moorland – I get caught up in a sense of adventure and exploration, of shelter and exposure, noticing different types of trees, birch and pine being two. I wonder if this is a place I could sleep out this coming winter, if I could put a tarp between these trees for the winter rain, if it would be sheltered enough in this spot. The landscape here is all hills and hollows, hidden holes and steep, unexpected drop offs, perhaps with a history of quarrying, it's hard to say now as everything is covered in the same layer of tough, lumpy moorland grasses.

I start to head home, finding my way back out through the hole in the fence, then the gap in the wall and down to an old cart track, sunken on the lower part, the upper, now a sheep track. The underground watercourses and regular, heavy rain, coupled with shallow rooted grasses, likely all contributing to the track's slow shift downhill.

I find a way up, which I know will take me to the 'Beardy Man', a name we inherited for a hill which, when viewed from our house, has the look of a man's face, as if the rest of his body is buried and he looks south towards hill and sky – brow, nose and mouth of rock, beard of branch and twig. As I approach him from behind, I see a bird take off in the distance – a raven. This is Ravenfield, where a pair of ravens hang out and seem to graze the field, almost like sheep. They are so sensitive, so wild, taking no chances by giving humans a very wide berth. I stop in the hope that he'll land again (it feels like a 'he') and I watch him circle round and land just below the brow of the hill in front. I sit and watch him watching me, just his head sticking up. We are both very much aware that we are watching each other. Then he jumps into the air and catches the wind, his wings beat lazily as he circles effortlessly round the trees, escaping my proximity but not my gaze. I stay with that raven as he rounds the trees, dips and flies west up the valley into the wind, unsettling magpies as he goes. I see him swooping in and out of the trees a quarter of a mile away – with loose, heavy wing beats - then disappearing somewhere into the middle of the woods. I have the feeling he was aware of me the whole time I watched and was still hiding from me as he landed.

I head back down towards home, grateful for the experience I just had, of what's there for me when I open up to it. I have the understanding that what I am experiencing is just as much part of me as an early morning dream, a conversation with a friend, a good meal or a day at work. As I walk back down the track, I experience the world in slow motion, as if I'm moving with the pace of the landscape itself. I stop because it feels weird, like I'm drifting downstream in a silent moment. I breathe it in and continue, feeling the connection I crave, an unspoken conversation, an insight I have opened up to in that moment. I feel the knots of resistance and confusion I took out with me loosen and I see the benefit that being open to the world around me brings. I feel at ease again and although I have no idea what just happened, I trust it entirely.

There's something about the ordinariness of everyday experience that can be astounding. Opening up to nature allows me to feel free in the moment and to not look for explanation even though I may go into nature seeking one. I see that my connection with nature sets me straight, or perhaps sets me off on a different journey of discovery, one in which I am both part of the scene and observing it, allowing nature to grow through me and into the moment of my experience.

We all do this even if we're not aware of it, or should I say it is done to us, or with us, even. Every day we observe the world we are part of as if we are disconnected from it, through what we've learned from hundreds of years of our exercising dominance over nature. We chose to step away from the land and to not hear the sound of the wild within, our calling and our healing. Now that we are in a world in crisis – climate change, as it's called – it's asking for culture change. We are cutting down rainforests and annihilating animal species like never before, plants and animals and people being part of the global balance, which had stabilised temperatures on this planet for many thousands of years. Yet, somehow, it seems like we can't relate to that, perhaps because our survival requires us to change more than we are comfortable with or maybe because we simply don't know what else we can do now we've worked out resources are finite when we thought they were endless. We are beginning to see that we are not just victims of our interpretation of evolution, using phrases like 'survival of the fittest' and 'dog eat dog' to allow us to do what we please - we are responsible for an entire world's well being.

But I'm getting ahead of myself. After all, this book isn't about climate change. This book is about a journey, an ordinary journey made by an ordinary person, someone who pulled himself out of his every day life for 29 days in order to start reconnecting with himself, his grief and the beauty and sadness of the world as he went. It's all nature; the people, the landscape he traversed and the plants and animals he saw, even the tarmacked roads he walked, the roar of car tyres on the tarmac and the smell of truck exhaust fumes - all nature. The thoughts he had along the way, the judgements, ideas, failures and learnings – all nature. It's the story of lives and experiences that shaped this man, bringing him to a point where he decided he *had* to open up. All of that, including the past he wanted to come to terms with and relationships he felt could not be healed. And this is how he remembers it.

Part One – Getting Lost

Place

He grew up in a beautiful place. He didn't know it was beautiful, but it was. He knew he loved it and felt free within its raw, natural power, as did many more. That land edged the Atlantic Ocean, absorbed many storms and had a way of swallowing people whole. Artists and musicians went to live there, people who wanted to experience basic living on the edge of the world. There was both pride and pain in being part of its rugged cliffs and coastline, which had taken boats, ships and local lives. It produced storytellers to share tales of hardship and union, of desperate times and sadness. Dingle was a hard place with a soft name. In the 1980s it felt cut off from the rest of the world.

The Search for Still Waters

A place of big skies, shafts of white sunlight through billowing blue-grey and white cumulus clouds, confidently proceeded, holding their own beauty and power. He grew up with wild storms, churning seas and salty dampness; watching wilful weather fronts slowly make their grey way east. Days of rain, mist from mountain to sea, lagoon-like potholes and rusty metal farm gates hung on great, stony gravel pillars, having nursed a mist and sea salt cocktail for decades.

Not a place of floods, the land had plenty experience dealing with rain, channelling much of it through its watery veins and arteries, towards the freedom of the Atlantic. The land would soak up the remainder, leaving a wet sponge to navigate - a welly sucking challenge, a mucky puzzle.

'The end of nowhere' was how he would sometimes jokingly describe Dingle, a small town, population of two thousand people, halfway along one of three peninsular toes on the south west coast of Ireland, stretching out into the Atlantic Ocean. Next stop America. A stunning place and a tough place in many ways. Fantastic for storms, he watched those big rollers coming in – an awesome sight and a world of sound. A place of raw, unspoilt nature, it got into a person, there's no doubt. It was possible to feel separate from the rest of the world, there. Seabirds were plentiful, grass capped sandstone cliffs and brown-gold sandy beaches defined the boundary between land and sea. On a warm summer day it was the most beautiful place in the world, the sun sparkling on the gently rippling sea.

He was in tune with that place growing up. He was privileged to be raised there because he got to experience nature the way it had been for millennia (although likely with more trees and wild animals, in the past), in a place unsullied by industry and pollution – it felt clean and clear there. This special space was an open playground of hills, cliffs, waves, rocks, sand and sea. He grew up a little over a mile from the beach and spent a lot of time there as a child, skimming stones, playing and being lulled by the washing, lapping tide. The scene was truly idyllic and dramatic, with beaches, sea then the mountains of the Iveragh peninsula on the other side of the bay. And behind, the Strickeen on whose peak, wispy grey clouds would rest to warn of rain and where long white rolls of 'ceo brothall' would accumulate in fine weather – a 'heat fog' condensing on the hills above, which confirmed the weather to be fine and settled.

People

Culturally, there was a palpable feeling that some kind of familiar magic was at work, like the place was alive with something. They felt their history lay behind, clear and comforting and what lay ahead may have felt just as certain. They knew the neighbours and their stories and there was this idea of connectivity to the lives of others - even if sometimes it contained judgement and half-truths. So, they knew people by their family and judged them by the actions of their ancestors. There was no escaping that. It was important to know that stuff; it was about connection, a deeper understanding. The ability to judge but also to have empathy with another if they came from familiar stock. This felt like an old way of being, kind of tribal.

They observed the weather, they talked weather. It was their foundation. He would often hear the men talk it out, this metaphor for connection and empathy, which might be interpreted as follows: "'Tis grand" = "How are you?" "'Tis" = "I'm doing alright, actually" or "Don't ask, life is pretty bad". Words were used sparingly, each conversation sparse in its mystery. This was a given, a habit and no outsider could penetrate that. Absent people might be referred to by a nod in their direction, i.e. where they lived or else simply "himself". Names were almost too direct a reference, something a stranger would use. Why use a name? It's not the person. For people who really knew each other and grew up together there was a quiet knowing. Like the wind, rain and land, their world and the people within it were known. He used to love listening to grown ups talk. He wouldn't find out much because they would often talk in their code but he was aware of their own brand of gossip - hard to grasp, like the wind. Words released like swallows from the nest, went flying over sheds to dance on the breeze, change shape, glide and return. And then silence - always part of the conversation. Space was both used and respected.

He remembers a particular moment in a field, looking out over the valley - a thick, grey, angular curtain of shower trailing downhill towards the sea, sun on the brown-green hill behind. Both men were regarding it as they spoke. The view was part of the conversation, there was purpose within the location. At ground level, wellingtons stood on grassy peaks atop deep, water-filled hoofholes. Remains of a stone-studded earthen ditch in a wonky line, once a boundary. A stillness in the air. A hint of otherness, of the magic of the land and their relationship with it. People, land and words, together. He got a sense of what was being expressed, of the low undertone within weather talk, within any outdoor talk, space given to the elements for their say. It may not be the same now. Connection to land and the elements changes.

Moving On

1980s rural Ireland was in a time of change. People *wanted* change, they wanted better education for the next generation so they would stay and be industrious in Ireland, rather than migrating or emigrating, which was common. Times were hard, farming and fishing were how most people in the locality made a living. Small farmers often worked tiny farms – some could exist having fewer than ten cows to milk and a patchwork of tiny, traditional family farms sat alongside larger farms.

For local farmers part of that change took the form of knocking ditches to make fields bigger. Ditches, where he grew up are boundaries between fields, built of earth, stone, trees and plants and, of course, the many birds, vertebrates and invertebrates that lived there. Ditches are a built up protrusion and not a drain-like thing as one might imagine. That is called a dyke where he grew up. The ditches were being knocked to make bigger fields, maximising the space to grow grass for grazing cows and to make silage harvesting easier. This was progress – a new and important way to farm. The beginning of progression into the world of higher yields had come, with little thought for the eco-system contained within those living ditches.

Old Ways

His home in the 1980s was, to some degree, still attached to the 'old ways'. The pace of life was pleasantly restrained. Farmers trundled around in small Massey Fergusons, wearing old suits, 'peaky' caps and wellingtons, winking with a customary, West Kerry tic as they idled by - perhaps on their way home after a few pints. He loved that greeting, the wink, it was warm and reassuring – far more wholesome than a raised finger or a wave, which because of the speed of cars they eventually had to resort to. Most farms were small, family owned properties at that time, tended by sons who became fathers, then grandfathers, often never leaving the homestead. There was security in connection with the land and the culture had built up around it.

Growing up he had space to play in the garden and to feel that freedom of the countryside, with wide ranging views of hills and the sea and on clear days, the mountain range of MacGillycuddy's Reeks could be seen to the east. Down the road a few hundred metres was the farmhouse his mother was born in and where his uncle and grandmother lived, at the family farm. That house was the centre for the family, for visitors from all over the world - an array of cousins came to stay there. 'The Yanks' they called most of them, collectively, and there was generally a visit planned by one of the American family descendants.

The Yanks

He noticed their loudness the most – their voices would cut through wall, floor and wind as if they had learned to communicate long distance, as if there was more space in between them in America, or they were used to living in large houses and would have to shout. His mother once asked "Why are Americans so loud?" The reply came instantly "You have to be loud in America to be heard!" The Yanks were an enlightened bunch, optimistic and upbeat, bringing an unfamiliar energy with them – it was hard not to like them. They often brought gifts for the kids – kites and outdoor games – fun things, things for throwing into rings, weighted at one end, stuff he'd never before seen. One day, in a moment of childhood frustration, he threw one projectile hard towards the house and it smashed a plate glass double glazed window – the biggest in the house. It was the most frightened he had been since his sister accidentally smashed the car windscreen with a rock whilst trying to rescue a football from a tree – a stunned panic washed over him as he stood, open mouthed, waiting for his mother to come out after hearing what could only be the chillingly amplified sound of a huge window cracking and hence the impossibility of a return to the relative peace of one moment before. He wasn't punished – he did that part to himself.

The simplicity of their lives in comparison to what appeared to be the sophistication of the Americans' existence made him confused. He wondered what America was like. In photos it looked still, with strange exotic trees and low walls, flowers and smiling people. Was it always like that? He played with cousins who held a different kind of fun than his school friends. He cried when they left, as he knew it would be a few years before he would see them again. They were family. They seemed upbeat and happy, open in a way he felt connected to. He noticed the difference between people where he grew up and the outsiders and wondered about a more hopeful world outside of where he lived.

Aoife

Aoife, his sister, was born with severe cerebral palsy. Her life would turn out vastly different to that of most people. After a birth complication, during which her brain was starved of oxygen, she was confirmed to have suffered severe brain damage. This was a devastating shock to the family and something that he, at eighteen months was somewhat unaware of. The first year of Aoife's life was taken up with her being severely ill, having pneumonia several times. His parents struggled and suffered with the ups and downs Aoife's arrival brought to family dynamics, with two small children already, to care for. It was mentally and physically taxing for them and must have been extremely difficult to cope with.

Getting Lost

After medical consultations it was considered wise to put Aoife into care at eighteen months of age. She then went to live in a home seventy miles away. In some ways, his parents lost a child and he, as a three and a half year old, lost a sister. His childish brain deduced that Aoife was not who she was meant to be and he assumed that's how the rest of his family felt. Something had happened to her that stopped the life she should have had, just minutes before she was born. Once this idea took hold, he could not accept her as she was but could only feel sad for who she might have been.

His childhood wasn't difficult or challenging in the way some people's is. There was nothing outwardly wrong. He was quiet and shy, but friendly. Sensitive. He would be called "too sensitive" many times in his life and it began when he was little. He felt a bit detached from others and sort of lived in his own, scared little world. He found many grown-ups to be scary. There seemed to be a split with the older people, many of them were kind and lovely, and others came across as mean and spiteful. Those ones often did not know how to communicate with him, or with children in general.

There was a feeling that childhood was something children were expected to push through so they could get to the important part of being a grown up and having grown up talk about serious things that children never got to hear. This was a point of conflict for the boy. There was mistrust around children, as if they had to be led and tightly gripped – especially within the education system.

The Search for Still Waters

When he was five he was shamed in front of the whole school by a teacher because he had thrown a sandwich in the bin. This kind of social conditioning was commonplace in rural Ireland. Not being aware of wrongdoing is normal for a young child, the concepts of 'right and wrong' themselves being a social construct.

Distinguishing between right and wrong or predicting how people were going to react to his behaviour would become a great challenge. There were rules but they were mainly subjective. He would have to work hard to understand everyone's needs and keep them happy. But he could not. So he took to hiding. He became the 'good boy' that he was expected to be so he would get approval – after all that's what those in authority wanted, but within he was scared of making the wrong move, exposing himself and being humiliated.

The little boy was in a confusing world – sensing expectations of behaviour, living with shame and the fear of being shamed, and with a sister who he felt was not who she was meant to be. He hid his sister from the world and hid his problems. He hid emotions, weaknesses and strengths – all were not enough for others to see, shameful and unimportant. Yet in some way he felt he was lucky in his life. He knew he loved and cared for the people around him. He felt much empathy and love although expressing that amongst his peers and role models, for example, didn't feel right or acceptable.

Some grown-ups looked upon children as underdeveloped versions of themselves and he found that difficult. All children were then treated as if they were the generic 'child', as if all were exactly the same and that individual personalities were some sort of wilful behaviour that was somehow acquired in order to spite the grown-ups, requiring discipline to 'tame' it. When he encountered people like this he would shy away, retreating into himself like a turtle or a snail, hoping he wouldn't be seen and criticised for his perspective and personality, for his 'soft' ways.

All he had to do was get through those times, on his own. He didn't ask for help. As he moved through time, he began to feel that there was something fundamentally flawed about him, something to be put right with education and discipline and tradition. He felt that, like his displaced sister, he wasn't who he was meant to be and he felt a sadness for that lost part of himself, which had retreated deep inside. Just like his sister, there was something wrong with him and he felt alone with it. He did not understand that he could talk about it or change anything, he just accepted it as him. Yet, inside, he had hope that all would be ok. He had family members who loved him and could see his sensitivity.

He felt sad about his sister's life, he even felt a sense of shame about her. He could not have what felt like a relationship with her, and only felt resentful and angry about her disabilities. "It's a shame." He would reflect, through the years, about what Aoife could have been like at five, ten and fifteen years old. Lamenting his 'lost sister', he felt alone with, and somewhat burdened by her condition. He fantasised and sometimes even dreamed about Aoife 'getting better', the possibility of her waking one morning, looking around, smiling and saying "Here I am." He remembers the excitement and hope those thoughts brought to him. It was visceral, a physical longing, especially when he'd had that recurring dream.

Trips to the care home Aoife was in were often tough. Sitting there as a little boy, writing on the steamed up window in the back of the car on those interminable, bumpy journeys on 1980s potholed, rural Irish roads, he felt the effort it took to go and visit his sister. Getting to the place he felt the heaviness of it all. The hard, echoing stairs and corridors, random shouts of residents reverberating around the building. He feared the seemingly stern staff, who were committed to doing the work of looking after the children - mainly over-worked nurses - and he was afraid of the other residents, not knowing whether or not they were going to attack him, with their loud yells and unpredictable behaviour. And then he would see Aoife, so quiet compared to most of the others, perhaps because her condition was more pervasive. She would lie there and he felt how vulnerable she was.

Those visits to Aoife's 'home' in Foynes were difficult, for a young boy trying to understand Aoife's condition, why she was in a hospital style ward with so many other children with similar conditions. It was scary, upsetting and saddening. It didn't feel right, nor did it feel real. He learned to detach from it, in some way, as the truth was overwhelming. He didn't have any explanation about Aoife's 'handicapped' (as it was then called) condition. As a five year old, he related to the word 'handy' as something positive and 'capped' as some kind of lid on the handiness. The word had a solid, plastic feel to it, a kind of friendly completeness.

When she came home he would sometimes lie on the floor next to her, getting down to her level to 'play'. Her moans, humming and different sounds were a puzzle to him but it was her way of being and communicating, even if he didn't understand it.

Ireland in the 1980s was a country struggling with unemployment and finding its feet in the new European reality. They were 'getting on with it,' through tough times and so were Aoife's carers. The carers, his parents, he and his other sisters were all left to handle the situation in their own way. That was the way. There was no education around it or support as far as he was aware.

Aoife was later moved to a home called St Mary of the Angels in Beaufort, near Killarney, only forty miles from their house, where she remained for the rest of her life. She was happy and well looked after there, finding her true family of carers – people who loved her and with whom she built lasting relationships, throughout her life.

The Importance of Being a Worker

He loved the farm and what it brought. He spent a lot of time on his uncle's small dairy farm, which was about a five-minute walk from his house down through the fields or on the single-track road called The Height. His uncle was generous and patient, Tom didn't have children of his own, so he felt like he could have a different time there.

The Search for Still Waters

His Uncle Tom would pass by their house on his way to the creamery (where he took the milk from his herd of fewer than 30 cows) every morning and sometimes, on summer mornings he would catch a lift with Tom as he passed by on his way to town. The shiny silver steel bulk tank hitched up to the back of the Ford Cortina, with its pleasingly square, reliable boxy lines and generally friendly, open appearance. He often felt that cars (and their owners) could be judged by the face (the front bit with the lights and grille) and the face represented a personality of some sort. The Cortina had a square-fronted, friendly face, with the occasional glint of determination, whereas a Ford Escort looked a bit nervous and startled, as if you'd have to hold its hand to get it on the road. The jaunt into town was a flavour of freedom. There would often be a bit of queuing outside the creamery, which was a chance for farmers to chat about the price of milk and whatever other coded gossip might have been going around at the time. He could not tune into that talk, but what he heard was again sparse and understated, like weather talk.

After emptying the tank, a spin around town to buy the Irish Times newspaper would ensue, which sometimes resulted in a choc ice for 'helping'. He would do the 'job' of getting the newspaper from Curran's shop and the payment would sometimes be that ice-creamy treat. It didn't always happen, either. His uncle's calloused fingers would dig around in the loose change of the car's seemingly bottomless coin reserve and that sound would spark off a great excitement and magic. There was possibility, expectation but not always the desired result. It was tantalising yet he was never disappointed when he didn't get that choc-ice.

There was, of course, more to that journey than just a spin in the beige Cortina and some milk delivery. It was an escape into town, a time where he felt a bit free and even important, sitting in the front of his uncle's car, seeing the world through the people his uncle knew, smiling at strangers for acknowledgement, feeling proud and important to be included. This induced a nameless enjoyment of youth, stepping into another world he didn't understand or even care to. The creamery ritual was never rushed. It was an established social event.

His Uncle Tom had a long view. It was as if he could see more than most, like he was wearing different life goggles. Perhaps without the stresses of children and providing he could spend time developing his sense of the world whilst working the land. He took his time with everything, evaluated how to go about moving a rock in a field or rebuilding part of his house. It seemed he could do anything and there was always enough time because he had worked it all out beforehand, thus making time inconsequential.

His uncle told him of the Well Field where in generations past they used its well as a water supply. It was in the middle of a field with a pallet thrown over it to stop cows from falling in. He felt that the pallet was not a respectful enough covering for this hallowed spot, but not strongly enough to ever mention it. He would walk down the steps of the underground chamber, which had an otherworldly, ancient feeling about it. He looked for signs or writing on the walls to see something of the past but all it held was an inky pool of water at its base, the steps disappearing into its dark reflection. Despite all this, it felt like the most mysterious place he knew, like an access point to the underworld and despite the obvious lack of depth he was drawn in deeper, past the puddle and the worn stone steps and into the ground where the past lay buried. His uncle told him of the ring fort in the Bóithrín Field, the next field up, and how there had once been people living there. Standing at the gate he would draw the outline of the ring fort and ask the boy if he could see it. He tried and willed himself to see it, but never could. He knew about fairy forts and curses and was a bit scared of them because he had simply been told that it was bad luck to remove all trace of them. People had died shortly after cutting down a 'fairy tree' or after knocking the ditch of a fairy fort. He could only imagine what his uncle saw and the relationship his uncle had with his land. He would walk his fields sometimes just to be there, climbing over ditches, feeling the land under his feet. His uncle told him about just stopping and looking around, about how it was important to 'stand and stare' as stated in the poem, *Leisure,* by William Henry Davies. People weren't meant to be busy all the time.

The Sea

The Atlantic was close, only a mile from his house and it was both vast and mysterious for him. As a child he would splash in the waves with his family and loved the aliveness of the sea (they never used the word 'ocean', the Yanks' word). The comforting, repetitive sound of the tidal lap brought him to a meditative state, it was trance-like and reassuring. It was a place he rarely ventured deeper into – he preferred working the land and feared the sea, in many ways – one of which being swimming. He had tried to learn on the tiny beach at Sláidin, attending the weekly lessons, in the occasionally cold and wet summer days, the rain sometimes pelting his shivering body as he stood, clutching a Styrofoam board for warmth, nodding to half-heard instructions. It was as if his body wasn't meant to swim, it felt too heavy for the water and therefore he gave up, thinking he would never be able to do it. The sea was vast and stretched endlessly out in front of him, its power both compelling and frightening. The frequent high winds and waves were not to be messed with – it was clearly a dangerous place. And there was the deep – the idea of getting pulled under and sinking forever into its airless mass was too much and made him stay away.

The voice of the sea was loud and ever-present. He feared the deep as he feared his own depths – the parts of himself he could not approach. The shame and sadness about his relationship with himself, with Aoife and everyone else lay somewhere out there in the depths of the Atlantic, lost like treasure. He wondered if others felt that way about relationships and connection, whether they too were desperate for deeper conversations or a sense of openness and freedom that felt impossible. He craved that connection in every interaction.

The Silage

From a very young age he was obsessed with farm machines and tractors – he didn't have the toys but was lucky enough to have the real thing to hand - and some of his earliest memories are of being in and around tractors. One particularly strong memory was of being on the tractor with his uncle, driving into the slurry pit and feeling very frightened because he was told the slurry pit was the most dangerous part of the farm. They called it 'a joyride'. It was simultaneously joyful and frightening, which strengthened its appeal. The apparent contradiction of the grown-ups' rules was dizzying – both naughty and amazing. Such were the cheap thrills of country life.

The silage was the social event of the year for him and, as he got older, he played a role in it. He revelled in the silage making. It was a magical time. A gang of men working big machines to perform an essential job - it all felt so important. When he was small, he sat in the tractor with whoever would have him, straddling the arms at the back or hanging on at the side where the door should have been. Kids were experts at hanging on to tractors, like baby chimps cling to their mothers.

The roads were pot holed and bone shaking. They had to match movements as the driver negotiated potholes, like moving with a boat navigating waves, for if he held on too tight, he was sure to bang his head or hurt himself unexpectedly on some exposed piece of metal framework on a Ferguson 168 or some such tractor. So he would have to sway back and forth, holding on, the occasional shout of conversation above the clank of the linkage and the humming Perkins engine. Even though the pain brought tears to his eyes when he hit his head, he knew better than to complain or 'let on', which may have brought doubt into the mind of the driver as to his toughness, and therefore merit as passenger. Not showing pain was an unwritten rule of the countryside of his youth. Many people around him were farmers and farmers' kids; they were tough and could work long hours and didn't complain.

For him, spending hours on a tractor felt like the best thing he could do with his time. He would hop on and off, when he was young, acting as liaison between his grandma and the workers, calling them in for dinner at one o' clock or bringing them tea and barm brack at four. It was summer and the silage generally had to be done in dry, sunny weather. A team of four or five men would do it – one cutting (usually reserved for the farm owner) and depending on the distance back to the yard, two or three 'drawing' - towing high railed trailers full of the cut grass back to the yard, where another would use their tractor and buckrake (a big fork-like loader at the front of the tractor) to spread the grass in the pit. Cutting the silage usually took around three days – that was three days of four tractors working on his uncle's small farm – so many machines meant overwhelming excitement and occasional breakdowns, which were just more excitement. On a warm summer's day the combined aroma of soil, cut grass, red diesel and hydraulic oil was something special - the aroma of freedom.

On silage days, each farmer would milk their cows in the morning, go to the creamery, then start on the silage, finishing in time to do the evening milking, then back again to work until dark. At the end of the day, they would gather in the cubicle shed in the yard and share a drink. There always seemed to be a wooden crate full of drinks in the shed at that time of year. Bottles of porter and lager maybe, tins of 'minerals'. They would all stand there in the near dark, the occasional draw on a cigarette lighting up faces – words sparse – an occasional burst of laughter. It felt weird to stand there in the dark with drinks, but it was special. A reflective moment at the end of a hard day's work. Community in action. It was the harvest; something old and deeply meaningful lay in those moments, the collaboration between neighbours and friends and essential work for the survival of the farm and the preservation of livelihoods.

In the late 1980s, more and more local farms used contractors to cut the silage and when the silage pit gave way to 'roundy bales' his uncle and neighbours decided to share the cost of the equipment and kept doing it themselves. At the beginning of the '90's, a second hand disc mower, baler, turner and wrapper were sourced from England and they continued to collaborate, saving money and keeping a key part of the farming tradition alive.

One day when at school, he was called out of class by the principal. "Your mother was on the phone" he said, "You need to go home as there is a family matter." 'Family matter?' he wondered to himself as he biked out the road on the warm spring day. They were short someone for the silage and he had to do it. For him that was the ultimate rite of passage, getting time off school to sit on a tractor all day, listening to tapes and smoking, when he could get away with it. He was elated as he hated school with a passion and, quite possibly, never felt so much joy as he did that day, in the fields, with the men, driving up and down in a tractor. That was it! All he needed.

The Spuds

When his Uncle Tom first showed him how to sow onions setts he was probably less than ten and keen to get involved in some way. Happy to leave him to it, Tom busied himself elsewhere. When he checked back on the work later on, he spotted that all the onion setts were sown upside down. He was so gentle and just laughed about it, pointing out the error and reassuring him it was fine, but he felt terrible about it nonetheless. He felt bad about a lot of things and was very sensitive to what he heard as criticism.

He grew up with 'the spuds' as an annual ritual, something that marked the seasons and was an essential staple crop for them. This was another learning from his uncle, a tradition he had kept going and one that most other farmers around them had given up, as it was time consuming and labour intensive. Starting with a bare bit of grassy ground in a corner of a field, in spring, the first ridge would be marked with a string line as a straight edge and scored along with a spade. The string line would then be moved along to guide the scoring of the opposite side, eventually producing a potato ridge half a metre wide and usually about twenty metres long. His uncle did most of that work, painstakingly scoring and turning over the sod to make several ridges – days of repetitive, methodical work he must have enjoyed.

His uncle had a potato mentor by the name of Dan Mháire who was in his seventies at that time. Tom must have invited him to grow his spuds in his plot and in return he got to learn from Dan. Tom used to say how Dan's spuds were always perfect and would study his technique – it was enough to have Dan there to observe his expertise. Dan dressed like a typical West Kerry farmer (suit and wellingtons) apart from one detail – he wore a black beret instead of the usual tweed peaky cap. He wore horn-rimmed glasses and had little tufts of white curly hair that puffed out from beneath his hat. His skin was surprisingly unwrinkled and he had a lightness to his character – he was a gentle man who smiled a lot and seemed to be in a pleasant, chilled out world of his own. At harvest time, Dan would show up on his 'High Nelly' bicycle, with a particular type of spade strapped to the crossbar. The loy spade was an important part of the potato harvest. A traditional, narrow spade, its blade was about five inches wide with a rounded end and a blackthorn knot as a lug, where the foot pushes it home. It was lightweight and caused less damage to the crop as it was harvested. He learned to speed his way through the ridges with this 'machine'.

A Fungicide was applied to protect the spuds from blight, which later was replaced by 'blueshtone', as it was called locally – real name copper sulphate, which was thought to be less poisonous than the fungicide. The potato famine was etched somewhere in their consciousness and although they could buy spuds if the crop failed, there was that feeling of threat from blight, affecting the tradition of growing their own supply. One year the crop suffered some blight - a powerful reminder to him of how nature can 'take away'. That was how it felt. It was easy to see how his ancestors, only a few generations before, had suffered and felt at the mercy of the weather and conditions in which they lived and farmed.

As he grew, he got time off school to harvest or dig the spuds. This usually happened sometime in early October. It was hard work but as the years went by, he was used to hard manual work and would dig the family's winter supply of spuds in a few days. That back stiffening work on a calm, warm autumnal day in the stillness of a field was a welcome change from the increasingly dull schoolwork and social setting of the Christian Brothers boys' school. All he had to do was use the tools in front of him, focus the mind on one task, often not having to speak to anyone all day. It suited him. Connecting with the land in front of him with a simple task that bore fruit. The knowledge that this was valuable work - he was feeding people, doing something practical and connecting with his ancestors through nature - motivated him. Sliding the spade into the ground with the aid of a foot on the lug, using the knee as a lever, the white or red of the skins bubbling up from beneath. There was mystery around what would be unearthed, their size and number, how the land simply grew the spuds *for* them. It was almost too easy - simple, but not easy.

The Outsider

He spent a lot of time outdoors as a child and that, combined with the enjoyment of hard work was a great focus for him in those days. He could hide in the work and feel the power of the world around him, which made sense to him. He had very little interest in school, his attention span shortening as he lengthened. However, he could sit on the beach and listen to the waves, walk for miles, sit on a tractor or do some repetitive, physical work task for hours on end without a problem. These were most important to him, yet at the same time he didn't feel drawn to farming as a career, performed poorly academically and in sport and generally felt like there was no career direction for him, outside of doing labouring work – which was the path he followed for many years.

As a teenager, his relationship with his family deteriorated. He could not communicate with them and felt it was somehow 'their fault', in that typical teenage way. Relationships became frayed and antagonistic for him and he struggled between the old ways of tradition, the rural Irish mind set and his own drives and need for self-expression. He knew he was shutting down to potentially meaningful interactions and that something about his life felt 'wrong', but he had no clear vision of what he actually wanted, so he remained shut down, mainly because he felt scared to interact with the world at large. It was as if he didn't feel important enough to have a future to work towards. He lived and breathed sadness - a 'head-hanging' sort of sadness, the kind tinged with shame, helplessness, guilt and regret.

He also had a quiet optimism. There was a knowing that everything would be OK despite his situation and how he chose to behave. He knew he was loved and cared for, but found it difficult to connect with that. He remained upbeat and although his negative thoughts were rampantly running the show, he felt that things would work out, a deeper feeling and a longing to experience that feeling lived within him. It was a kind of trust that there was a better plan for him, a faint glow through the layers of his worries. Where did that trust come from? He did not know, but it was barely a whisper, not enough to motivate him.

He cultivated himself as an outsider, gradually detaching from almost everyone around him, for fear of being hurt. He began to live in his mind, not in the world, and meaning changed for him, seeing society as something he was outside of — something broken, disaffected and abusive. He had been bullied over the years, as many had, and felt like he didn't belong. He didn't understand what he had to do to fit in. In an all boys school he tried to connect with others, but often they were too busy being young boys, while he was seeking deeper connection, some kind of truth or a 'way in' to friendship. This approach often didn't end well for him, so he ditched that in favour of becoming 'hard to reach' himself. He struggled at the game of being a teenager, of teenage banter and one-upmanship and so he hid. He was either 'too open' or became guarded and that kept him feeling alone and vulnerable. He sometimes felt he could see others' pain and fear, could see them hiding, like he was.

He began to see his peers as a threat and foolish; socialising and drinking – all of that seemed childish and pointless to him – merely games people were playing with each other, blindly disrespectful of who they really were. He rarely had the courage to ask girls out, even when experiencing painful feelings of love. He was a spectator, not a player. He longed for closeness – for romantic involvement, for touch, arousal and a depth of connection he felt, but could not bring himself to open up to.

So he withdrew and lived within, compensating by convincing himself that nobody was good enough for him, judging harshly and cruelly anyone who didn't meet his self-imposed standards. He ended up feeling utterly and completely alone.

His participation in society became cursory and he mostly hid behind pleasantries and shallow interactions. His fear of being judged and criticised - especially by his peers - was so great that he avoided doing that which would open him up to such things. He avoided sport, academic life, socialising, expressing his opinions and standing out in any way. He side lined himself from his community, but stood in judgement of all. He had finally shut himself off from the world and even fleeting moments of connection with others often left him feeling exposed and confused. He sought out other outsiders for solace and connection, sometimes kind and sometimes edgy people on the fringes. They recognised something in each other, maybe the deep feeling or need to feel OK and accepted for their difference.

Like Waves

He walked and cycled for miles alone, enjoyed throwing stones – a pastime he and his father would do together, at the beach at Dún Síon, where the dunes and beach grass sloped down to the soft, golden banked up sand, which held the odd piece of driftwood, discarded fishing flotsam or occasional ancient, scarred piece of plastic bottle or tin can. The beach held many secrets including the bottleneck entrance to a shallow tidal lake – a narrow, fast moving bit of water, a forbidding current which would fill and empty out with each tide, making it dangerous to swim in – people had tragically drowned there in the dangerous current. The narrowest point of the estuary being about thirty feet wide, fairly shallow and, looking inland one could see the entire area as a sandy beach surrounded by fields, which then appeared as a lake when the tide was in. Seabirds were plentiful; gulls and oystercatchers, curlews sinking their long, curved beaks into the soft, muddy sand – and them, stones in hand, poised for the next throw – silently competitive, seeing who could reach the rocky opposite shore of that tidal river, skimming stone after stone, slowly advancing, scanning the corrugated sandy surface at low tide for the ideal stone amidst an endless supply, apparently only replenishing as time went by. It was all theirs. Despite their difficulties, this was their space and time together, the sound of the sea, the satisfying, muted clack as

33

thrown stone met the seaweedy rocks on the opposite side. How the west wind affected both distance and direction, sometimes snatching a stone from the sky mid throw and at other times catching it and taking it further than was felt possible. Man, boy, wind and stone in a quiet game at the edge of land and sea.

Together the family would often have Sunday morning adventures, exploring the rocky coastline, places with names like Nancy Brown's Parlour and Fothar Na Manach, Bull's Head and all the beaches of the area. It was rare for them to meet people on their walks and adventures – the beaches were empty apart from in high summer, few walking routes or footpaths existed, so they often had to find their own way.

Stepping out of the cultural mould in the early 1990s took a kind of courage he did not possess. The old ways seemed inevitably caught up with complex emotions, religion and idiosyncratic behaviours. However, with every hidden path there were hidden gems to find - beautiful moments of connection with people, moments of unquestioning openness and generosity from people. There was desire for something different and new and the fear that brought with it. A lot had already changed since his mother's childhood only forty years before, when children walked barefoot to school and poverty was commonplace, Dingle was a mainly cut off from the rest of the world. Their rural culture had remained mostly unchanged for centuries, hardship was commonplace and accepted, not commented on or wallowed in.

By the time he was a teenager European money was flowing and long-held cultural traits were beginning to dissolve with the onset of a more liberal, integrated European agricultural present. The old ways were being preserved through the Irish language, but the mind set with its connection to the land and lore was fading, along with the less desirable traits of control, conservatism and secrecy, between the church and traditional family ways.

Music Escapes

When they got a car with a tape player, in 1988, they started listening to music from the sixties that his dad was into. The Beatles and The Beach Boys were the most played and sung along to. They had great journeys with those tapes, singing along and a lifelong love of pop melodies and vocal harmonies was tattooed into his consciousness.

He took to spending more time alone when he was a teenager, walking the roads or cycling and listening to music. He put his headphones on and he was gone, the louder the better. He didn't have to interact or engage – it suited him to be in his own world. Music saved him in some way. He wasn't so into traditional Irish music, it reminded him of the oppressive feeling culture he was growing up in. He also had scary (for a sensitive five year old) experiences at the traditional Irish Music and Arts school 'Teach Siamsa.'

Little outside of the mainstream was accessible to him where he lived, as far as he was aware. He listened to bands like U2, EMF, The Pixies, Pavement, Nirvana, Therapy? and The Prodigy, whose album 'Experience' set fire to his mind in a way he had never before experienced. He went to Tralee on the thrice-daily bus to buy that album after having heard one of their tracks on a compilation. He removed it from its plastic wrapping and put it in the Walkman. It was like rocket fuel, exploding with power and from the first seconds the vibe was urgent and all consuming, unleashed through electronic instruments, sounds he'd never heard. Beats that blew his mind. He looked around him on the bus feeling so high he could not believe he was still in the same vehicle as the rest of the people, who were just sitting there, swaying and bobbing with the bus's lolling pace. He was convulsing within, he had molten lava flowing through his veins. How could they not feel it?

His neighbour had a caravan on their driveway they used as part of their B&B and some kids from Dublin stayed there, leaving behind a tape. His friend played the tape, which again broke his brain somewhat – it was the N.W.A. album "Niggaz' 4 Life". It opened up another dimension to him, just like The Prodigy had. It was so crude in many ways – demeaning to women yet sort of like an ironic x-rated comedy - to a rural Irish teenager, it was perfect fodder - holding the magic of a world he had never before even heard of – the world of rap and fat beats, recycled, looped grooves and rhythmical words stimulating his brain, making him feel alive. The Beastie Boys did the same. Rap pushed back against the norm, a little secret world of cheeky, off the wall shouty boys who didn't seem to care what they said - perfect for the lonely, old school Catholic Introvert, living on a quiet peninsula on the edge of the world.

Getting Lost

He didn't know what that music was doing to him but he wanted more. He got into 'rave' music, finding occasional compilations. Again, the beats tugged at him, repetitive and pulsing, something primal. He had no idea of the cultural movements and musical history that lay behind any of the music he listened to but that didn't matter. He felt he wanted to be a drummer, setting up a 'kit' in the crumbling old garage out the back of their house. It was made of bits of wood and paint tins. Something was awakened within him through music but, as with so many other aspects of his young life, he kept his passion mainly a secret, mixing with a few indie kids but mostly afraid of being judged for his musical taste and he did not pursue playing the drums until he left Ireland. It wasn't worth it.

His problems were his own but perhaps also cultural, borne out of centuries of resistance and resilience, of not feeling free and having to keep culture under wraps. It was as if some part of him suffered that loss and it became his personality. He was, after all a product of that culture, of that time and place and felt overwhelmed by it all. Music was a route to freedom.

Part Two – The Ingredients of Awakening

Fifteen Years Later

Near the town of Leverburgh, on Harris in the Outer Hebrides there is a tiny museum in a field, by the water, dedicated to the life and works of ornithologist and naturalist William MacGillivray. The MacGillivray Centre is a tribute to the artist's time living on Harris. He was born in Aberdeen but spent much of his childhood in that rugged, rural Atlantic idyll, a couple of hundred years before. He went there in 2010 with his wife Beth and dog Suzie, braving the harsh August weather, which consisted of frequent showers, rough seas and the occasional wave of midges when it was calm. They played on Harris's empty, bright gold beaches, running down vast sand dunes, marvelling at the Atlantic, the dark brightness of the sea and its foamy crashing waves – formidable yet reassuring. They camped in their vegetable delivery van.

MacGillivray's story captured him, especially when he learned that at the start of each year of University, MacGillivray would walk from the Outer Hebrides to Aberdeen, and then back to Harris for the summer, where he lived and worked on his uncle's farm. He loved the sound of this. Then he saw, within this tiny museum, that MacGilivray had once written a book with the modest title: *A Walk to London.* Despite that walk having taken two hundred years before, something about MacGillivray's life, that place and his journey hooked him in.

He bought the book, feeling like he had found treasure in a most unlikely place. The premise of MacGillivray's walk was to make the 828 mile journey from Aberdeen, across the Highlands and then on to the Natural History Museum in London, which he had previously only read about. It was written in 1819, in archaic language and was a journal both of the flora and fauna he saw, along with the highs and lows of the journey south. For example, he wrote of his knapsack made of thick oiled cloth: "This machine which cost me six shillings and sixpence contains the following articles" and he goes on to describe a great amount of art materials, one set of clothes and a glass for drinking fresh water from streams as he went, a practice which was frowned upon at the time. MacGillivray slept at inns on hay mattresses, ate a lot of bread and milk and sometimes put his head down for the night in a ditch, in the rain.

After reading this obscure and entertaining book, full of idiosyncratic descriptions of places, plants, people and their behaviour, he held the idea of doing some kind of similar journey for himself. He allowed MacGillivray's story in, he could identify with the Atlantic coastal upbringing, the relationship with his uncle, the feeling of living close to the land and its people and with MacGillivray, who appeared to also be a bit of a loner.

He had never been interested in adventure, taking physical risks or even long walks before he read that book. He was a mostly unadventurous and quite scared person who had heard somebody talk of the Camino Di Santiago when he was in the pub having a few pints once, but hadn't given it any thought. That sort of trip was for someone else, someone who deserved it. The book was a kind of revelation, the idea of a possibility, previously unthought of by him. A walking journey, an ordinary person in his own little fantasy world, getting somewhere in his own unique and ordinary way.

Rock Bottom Riser

On the 23rd September 2011 he and his wife Beth sold their business. It was a small fruit and veg business and the time had come to move on from it. They had built it from scratch for the previous four years, with all its joys and stresses. They had been feeling tension in their relationship – almost every conversation they had was based on the business, leaving them little time to connect like they had before. They had also been trying for a baby for years and that process was becoming stressful and fruitless. They were starting on the medical fertility route, which felt daunting and heavy.

Sitting in a clean, glassy office in Manchester, on a chrome and leather chair, he felt awkwardly out of place on the day they signed over the business to its new owner. They felt precious about their 'baby' and used to joke that it was their 'first born' as they started it only a couple of months after they got married. The office was the opposite of the pleasantly grubby world of the veg box business, and he felt cynical towards it. He judged the pretentious veneer of chrome and faux leather and how it contrasted with the messy rollercoaster of local food systems, vegetable procurement, the love of food and the challenges of running a fresh food home delivery business. That day was strange for another reason though. It was also the day Aoife died.

His mother phoned early that same morning to deliver the news (she never rang his mobile), so it was definitely going to be about Aoife, as she had been ill for a few months. After the call he stopped and looked around him, at the bedroom in the rented house on Princes Road. The old sink in the corner, the dark-stained floorboards with big chunks missing, woodchip wallpaper and the Victorian doors, skirting boards and architraves all a uniform glossy beige, painted, he imagined, about twenty years before. The bedroom door was open and down the hallway he heard the intermittent splashing of Beth showering, studied the Victorian woodwork and the ominous dark blue hallway carpet - a dependable dog hair magnet for Suzie's shedding. He looked around between one feature and the next, as if some deeper context would reveal itself, as if he were being shown a secret meaning within the scene that was just outside of his grasp. He felt *there* in a way that was unusual – time had slowed in some way. He didn't feel sad. He didn't know how he felt, that was the truth.

The Funeral

When they arrived back in Ireland the wake was magical, proper Irish style. It was a celebration, Aoife's body was laid out in the sitting room, the neighbours had made cakes and food, and the house was buzzing - full of people having a great time. He felt grateful for the community spirit, for the people looking after them. The food, which the neighbours had quickly made appear, felt like the glue that held it all together and contrasted well with the previous day's business deal. His parents seemed in good form, which he was happy about. Neighbours told them to sit down, brought them food and drinks and chatted warmly. There was something bewildering about it all. This celebrating felt at odds with his feelings, but at the same time too warm and open to be ignored. He felt a mixture of joy and confusion. 'What was the point of Aoife's life?' he started to wonder, crudely. 'She's gone now, that's it, but what am I left with?' He felt numb, but also recognised that people were celebrating Aoife's life.

At her funeral service he delivered some words about how Aoife was someone he had learned from, about how she was there to teach something to everyone she came into contact with - words he felt compelled to use, but could not see what they meant for him. He felt detached from Aoife and wondered what their relationship as siblings meant – he saw it as a disconnected relationship, as if he never knew her, never bothered to get to know her. Like it was too much to do so.

When Aoife died she had spent her life being cared for, a life that was in essence like everyone else's but in terms of society was completely different to most. Did she know who she was? Did she understand complex language and concepts? Did she feel trapped inside her body when almost everyone around her was able to control theirs? This he never knew for sure. When he saw her lying in her coffin, looking small and pale, he knew something was finished. A certain, deep tension was released – something he had felt for decades. The everyday tension of knowing Aoife was alive and the effect she had upon him, that he couldn't pick up the phone and talk to her like he could with both his other sisters, that when he went home he would reluctantly visit her and a great, deep sadness, an inner conflict would begin to rise, like some boiling mess, not understood in any way. He didn't know if it was his fault. He felt terrible though, a deep sadness about his relationship with Aoife ground away at him and because he felt it when he was around her, he blamed her for it, as if she, who couldn't walk, talk or cast aspersions had done it to him.

When he went to visit her in later years he would always take her outside, into the grounds, in her wheelchair. He would push her and quietly sing into her ear, leaning close to her head as they walked. Whatever tune came into his head. Sometimes he would walk quickly with her or even run as it seemed that she liked it. They both enjoyed it. Visits to her were so full of intense emotion, all he wanted to do was run away. It was like a terrible injury that was being aggravated or what he imagined a PTSD reaction to feel like. Almost like an emotional crisis.

When she died he wanted to cry and grieve and weep and feel – something. But he didn't. When he saw her in her coffin he didn't cry. When she was lowered into the ground he watched, as if disconnected, like he was watching it happening to someone else, unaware of his own feelings. He was quiet and felt quiet within, reverting back to the old familiar questions, which had occupied him for decades 'What is the point of life?' 'Why are we here?', 'Who am I?' and 'What does this mean?'

Those questions would stay with him and, without him realising it were unconsciously turning the cogs, creating a plan for him. His relationship with Aoife, which he thought to be in the past, would open up for him in a way he was not then aware of.

Gut Feeling

Within a few months of her death, he realised that he was beginning to forget his sister and in some sense he was putting it all behind him, in a neat way. He was aware that he had not felt the grief of her passing, nor had he taken time to feel what it meant for him.

In the meantime, his wife bought him a book. It was called 'Wild – An Elemental Journey' by Jay Griffiths. In it Griffiths discusses how she had had depression for many years and was helped through taking Ayahuasca in a controlled environment. He didn't identify with the depression at the time but he knew that there was something not quite right – that he had yet to discover the person he was supposed to be and a bit like reading MacGillivray's book, Griffiths' journey also drew him in. He was intrigued and decided to follow it up with some research.

He was drawn to the research with energy and excitement. He began to look online, reading every article and watching every video he could find. He watched videos of people retching their guts up in jungle huts, eating plain rice and vegetables for weeks before the 'medicine journey' to cleanse their bodies, shamans chanting mysterious mantras. He read about fake experiences and abuse and a confusing, contradictory world of positives and negatives around the controversial 'jungle juice.' He read about people who were possessed by demons or had picked up bad spirits, which had to be released, terrifying visions, people reliving past trauma, desperate people who wanted to be healed. And despite all of that he thought 'This is for me.' He even completed a foundation Spanish course at the Cervantes Institute in Manchester and was planning on continuing with the study. The 'curanderos' or South American Shamans who guided the Ayahuasca journey would do so in Spanish, so he could be ready to release the spirits, battle his demons, and hear the shaman sing his song of release and recovery without a translator. He was building up for something major, life changing and new!

Within three months of selling the business they found out Beth was pregnant, he had a new job, joined a band and another three months later, went on tour. The plans for the jungle trip were shelved as having a family was the next thing to plan for. He went back into his world of distractions. He didn't have to admit to himself that he was depressed and anxious, that he felt there was something deeply wrong with him or that he knew he should be someone else, someone better than he was. These mind states coloured his reality – he saw achievements as accidents, he was disconnected from feeling good about himself and his life. Drinking helped him stay that way, it dulled him just enough that he didn't need to delve. He could stay feeling bad about himself and his life instead of taking action.

His sister was gone and life could become normal after being strange for thirty-three years. Part of him believed that would happen. The same part that dreamt of Aoife waking up one morning and being 'normal', waking up from her illness and recognising the joy and excitement of life, the laughter and fun of being a child – that Aoife was OK, as she was moments before her birth, which left her brain starved of oxygen, before the slow dawning on his parents that they had a very sick baby, who then spent the first year of her life fighting for her to live – and she pulled through. She showed a resilience to be alive in this world in that form that he, as a child, could not accept in a way he could not explain or even be aware of. Aoife was now not her physical being, which caused him to wonder if somewhere she was still in existence beyond her body. He cursed what he felt like was his damaged mind and his twisted emotions and wondered if somewhere within himself he was actually already free. In general, his thoughts told him he was no good, even bad and he felt like a bad person, as if he had committed a terrible crime. His idea of himself as bad led him to believe that most other people must also be rotten in some way, that they didn't mean what they said, or just pretended to be his friend and so he looked for ways to distrust people, as he had as a child. Could he put Aoife behind him?

Grounding

When his beautiful daughter was born he suddenly longed for more meaning in his life. He wanted to be a better person for *her*, someone she could look up to – anyone but the failure he felt he was. He changed jobs again, this time working at an urban market garden, only a few miles from Manchester city centre – a rare green gem in the urban and modern industrial city. Here, he worked hard and had the space he realised he needed. He worked with people, plants and soil, with the seasons and in all weathers as that was what was required, tending vegetables and being part of a market garden business. It reminded him of home, working the land, feeling that space. He started to, once again, notice more details in nature, he raised plants from seed, learned from his colleagues about how the business worked and helped adapt and grow it. As the seasons went by, each was completely different and there was no escaping the feeling of progress and learning.

It was hard work but winter was quiet and as both the plant growth and business slowed he embraced the rhythm of that. The inevitable yet gradual rise of spring, with its false starts and chilly interludes, the intensity of summer with successional sowing and planting of salads, of harvesting, selling and soil preparation, of crop failures and frustrations, of the slow learning from one year to the next. He let go of the failures and successes of the manic days and the tiredness and stiff muscles of summer, of the accumulated exhaustion and waning autumnal energy, the satisfaction of another season of hard work, hilarious moments and even disappointment. Each season was unique and beautiful and fleeting. He worked with kind people, had fun and felt supported.

Most of spring was spent slowly filling up the plantraising area with new trays of seedlings, bringing them through the colder parts of spring, which often entailed covering baby plants with sheets of plastic or bubble wrap, ready to plant out as soon as it became warm enough. Then summer came with its never-ending routine of sowing and harvesting – all they had to do was keep up with their winter plan.

The work calmed him, gave him a sense of purpose. He could understand the process clearly, of people, plants and land. A perfect loop of existence, nothing else was needed. He was 'home' in a way he had not felt since the days on his uncle's farm. "Farming is freedom", he would say to himself, as he planted a bed of lettuce or weeded the spring onions on his hands and knees, filthy fingered and child-like. He felt his connection to the earth grow and as he began to put down roots, he reflected on what was familiar about the work he was doing – the importance of his connection to nature, to farming and the land. That was what he did as a child – not exactly that, but in some form. Working the land. It was something to occupy his body and mind, which suited him. He began using that freedom to ask deeper questions and he began a journey inward. Reconnecting with the land gave him the opportunity to reflect in the way he used to - a way that brought some balance into his life.

One weekly summer job was building a miniature, hooped tunnel for brassica salads. This was achieved through using a large metal bar to punch holes through the soil on either side of the bed, holes that would hold the plastic hoops in place. As he punched those holes and worked the land he realised that his mind was becoming quieter, that he was soothed by the work and for the first time in years he felt space around himself. He would 'stand and stare' as his Uncle Tom, who had died a few years before had suggested, and felt that deeper connection with the land, time and himself. Standing there, taking a momentary break from hard work, absorbing the scene, tuning into sound and his visual field so completely that at times it all felt perfect - one timeless moment in which everything was contained – past, present and future, no matter.

Each week there was a plan for roughly what to sow and plant and from then on it was up to them and how they could keep up with the pace they had set themselves. As the season went into full swing there was a simple rhythm of sowing, plant care, harvesting, planting and weeding. As summer progressed the work would rise to a crescendo of endless, fast paced days and giving in to the madness of it seemed the only way to cope. They would 'lose it' for weeks on end, laughing hysterically and becoming involved in their own nutty little world of games. Coffee, biscuits and cake for energy boosts and the feeling of pure achievement were driving them on through long days of hard work and inspiring action.

That plan was carefully devised in the depth of the cold season - far from summer's intensity - when the cold wind, like a malicious giant ripped at the polytunnels' plastic jackets and rattled the whole glasshouse like a toy. They would cautiously look up from their winter harvesting work with the fear that shards of glass might rain down. Winter, when they spent time reading and going on holiday, was when they also planned the following summer's work. It was a simple process of moving with the seasons, allowing themselves to work with the growing space, making the most of the relationship between them, the land and the market.

A Way In

One winter he bumped into a friend who told him where he could have an Ayahuasca ceremony – hosted by a woman who herself had felt great pain and loss in her life and who had devoted her time to helping others. "Ayahuasca will only give you what you're ready for" she told him. He was more frightened than he had ever been in his life, the idea of surrendering to this force of nature. But he was desperate and sad, he wanted to feel alive and had had enough of being trapped in his thoughts, which told him he was worth nothing. He knew there must be a way to change his depressed state and he was desperate for that. His daughter, wife and his own life needed this change, they needed this man who felt scared and pathetic and like a failure to not be trapped in his own doomy existence any longer.

On his way to the ceremony he feared the wave of grief that might envelop him. Because he'd read and watched stories of people who'd gone to these sessions to eradicate demons, break 'unforgiveable' chains of behaviours such as addiction and crime – he felt the pressure and fear of 'getting it wrong.' People brought with them the sort of behaviours that can come from childhood abuse and trauma and can grow into the idea that the person is essentially bad and unlovable. He'd even heard of people who had had cancer cured through using that stuff. But were his problems enough to be healed or were they too big? He found it difficult to value and evaluate his own experience. He was stuck on trying to figure it out, which was his way. He didn't like trying things, he'd rather think about it and find reasons not to do it.

What is this mysterious medicine, this 'jungle juice', this 'drug', which is loved, hated and feared by so many people? Plants. Perhaps these plants are, as one man told him, eighth dimensional beings, here to help people evolve, but whatever they are, they work to stimulate healing, especially for those for whom healing feels like somewhere they may never reach. Two different plants, whose combination allows an experience which can alter perception very quickly, can help that person see things about themselves, others and the world, they had not thought of – detaching them from their everyday experience for a moment - bigger picture thinking it could be called. Plants, which have been used by Shamans in the jungles of South America in the time before Europeans came, ridiculed them and their culture and stole their resources. Plants, which were discovered through trial and error to have a most extraordinary effect on the brain.

Within the Ayahuasca space there were people to help and hold one's hand if needed, there was beautiful music and song to accompany people on their journey. He looked around and could see some people who looked like children, dancing around in excitement at the prospect of their evening's connection. He judged them harshly though, sensing they were afraid of him. Seeing that they were avoiding his eyes, he felt more disconnected than he had known – was there freedom out there for him? Was it possible for him to go beyond the prison of judgement, shame and self-torture he had built for himself? He didn't know, but he had decided to take a leap. He then looked around at the quieter people, like himself. Those who were perhaps also suffering in some way, and like him, were perhaps disconnected from the world around them in a way they too could not understand. He felt the calm in the room and felt supported by it. He felt the shame that led him there, the anxiety and fear that permeated much of his life. He desperately wanted to trust the trip he was about to go on.

The journey itself was like nothing he had previously experienced, he was both fascinated and afraid to let go, the intensity of the medicine taking his consciousness from its seat of judgement and fear, deep into his physical body - or out into the universe, it was hard to know. He travelled to places unknown although he still had the distinct feeling that it was within himself, as if he were the centre of this journey and he began to trust that. He did not have demonic visions nor did he find out that he was rotten inside, in some way, as he had feared.

Part of the journey consisted of the actual words "essential maintenance is being carried out!" echoing repeatedly within his mind, like a supermarket tannoy announcement, making him chuckle, as if he was part of a cartoon or a film and it was all a bit of a silly joke. He heard his name being called every hour or so from deep within, in rotation, as if he was within a planetary cycle, which revolved once an hour. The next time his name was called he'd had another world of experience which had taken him away from his idea of himself, this static, stuck broken self, and had experienced a deep feeling of 'otherness' taking place. The fourth or fifth time he heard his name called out, he had to focus hard on it as he tried to remember his identity in the world. This experience took him further and further from his concept and idea of himself. The final time he heard his name come round on the cosmic loop, he tried to remember who the name belonged to – was it someone he knew from his past? He had disconnected from his identity, even if just for one moment.

When he opened his eyes he connected with a purpose to everything that was occurring before him, it seemed as though it was all planned and like he had connected with a knowing that there was the possibility of feeling like things were meant to be the way they are. He was experiencing 'the present moment' in all its perfection.

The ceremony had given him the opportunity to detach from his idea of himself, from his identity, which was loaded with shame, sadness, with a lively undercurrent of fear. It was a chance for him to let go of the ego for a few hours and experience life without the sadness, anxiety and feeling like he was judging everything he and others did to check if 'everything was OK'. And as it turned out, everything *was* OK without the judging, anxiety, fear and sadness. He felt a freedom he could not remember having felt before. He had experienced the peace of simply being, the joy of the moment and, even though it was fleeting and he slowly returned to his regular self and ways afterwards, he had been shown that there was hope for him to feel happy, to get better – to forgive himself for what he carried so much guilt and shame about.

He had excitement, but did not know what to do about it – his life had not changed and he realised it was up to him to do something in order to feel change – do something for himself, for his life, in a way he never had since leaving Ireland. Sure, he had worked in food and played music in bands, fallen in love and had a child, yet his own self-development and awareness within it all lay neglected – he knew the world of work and was beginning to know his own family and most of his socialising had been based on the 'work hard play hard' ethic, with booze and escape the key ingredients. Doing low paid, stressful work, drinking a lot of alcohol and feeling connected to the others who were up for doing the same. There was nothing wrong with that of course, but it had become a habit, just as the negative self-talk had, just as the decades of feeding the sadness and disconnection from himself had been.

Deep Water

Back in Manchester, one day in the glasshouse he had a brainwave. Knowing that facing his fears was important, he asked himself "What am I most afraid of?" A clear answer came back within seconds – "Deep water." He was surprised at this simple answer and wanted something more profound so he cast about for a deeper, more meaningful, more perfect answer, but none came. He needed to learn how to swim, like he had tried, but gave up on as a child. To be able to swim in deep water would not only be a service to himself, but to his little daughter – it meant he could take care of her in deep water, therefore becoming a more responsible father, whilst learning a life skill.

Then he remembered the cold swimming lessons of his youth and more lessons in the indoor swimming pool at the Skellig Hotel. Mouthfuls of putrid, chlorinated water, the smell almost overwhelming as he held a styrofoam board out in front and kicked like mad. Facefulls of others' splashes. Breathing in gulps and gasps. A friend's birthday party where they went to a swimming place in Tralee. A sixty mile round trip in the dark back of a Toyota Liteace van, bouncing through potholes and unexpected turns. He was shy and scared, especially of water, feeling frightened, genuinely confused as to why everyone else seemed to be enjoying themselves. Swimming pools were threatening and smelly, echoey, slippery deathtraps, subtly pulling him into their depths.

Arriving at his first lesson as a grown-up was truly frightening. Not only was he going into the deep pool in Stockport leisure centre, he was admitting his ineptitude to a guy in his twenties he had never met before who probably swam like a dolphin. The coach, Harry Needs asked how he felt. He replied weakly, "Nervous?" he felt submissive and a bit stupid but there he was. They went through some simple routines and after the first lesson he felt relieved and not as thick as he had beforehand. This was half the battle. Harry demonstrated how to bear down into the water, which lifted up his middle, quickly fixing his thirty-year-fear of being a human anchor.

By lesson three he successfully swam across the deep part of the pool for the first time. What a feeling! At thirty-eight years of age he had achieved something most people do by the age of nine, something that he had spent most of his life just procrastinating about, and the sense of achievement he felt from that simple action opened up his imagination in a new way. When he had completed his third lesson, Harry gave him a postcard signed by his then wife, Olympic gold medallist Rebecca Adlington, which read "Alan, good luck with your swimming." This too made him feel like a nine year old, but by then he didn't care. He was able to acknowledge that he had achieved something big for himself and was very happy, partly because he overcame feeling stupid for not being able to swim. He was also in a state of shock at how easy it was for him to do. All those years of being afraid and wondering what it would be like to not be afraid and he had put a big dent in his biggest fear in a very short time. It actually felt easy.

The Undergrowth

At work he began to explore the concepts of 'self' and 'thought' and how they were connected – so often he felt like a seething mass of emotional confusion, but he knew he had to try and understand it all better. He was listening to an audiobook called 'The Untethered Soul' as he worked building a mini salad tunnel and came across a self-inquiry exercise, originating from Hindu sage Ramana Maharshi. The idea of the exercise was to ask "Who am I?" over and over, each time going a little deeper. This was a question he had asked himself a lot in his life, having often felt like he didn't belong or wasn't meant to be there. He had always felt there was a deeper part to him he couldn't reach and that's who he really was. As the exercise continued, it progressed to "Am I my mind?" and "Am I my thoughts?" At this he stopped his mini-tunnel building, putting down the iron bar he was using to punch the holes and a moment of realisation came upon him. "I am not my thoughts", he ventured. "My thoughts are not who I am." Looking up at the sky he saw the space around him. He had recognised the space around his thoughts before but hadn't considered its significance. He recognised something he had in some way always felt but could never put into words. Something deep and groundbreaking had happened. A wave of relief washed over him as he sat down on the bare soil – a knowing that all the shame, guilt and darkness he felt inside were not permanent and unchangeable, as he had felt. This one idea opened him up to a world of possibility for himself and his future. He could change his thoughts and was not cursed for life with his burden of a broken mind. He could give himself space to actually feel ok in.

The alchemy of outdoor work coupled with having a daughter had brought him to life in some small way. He began to wonder what he could do next for himself, for his own life rather than for a job or a social movement, as he had mainly been doing for years. Something good, something big, the likes of which he would never do in his regular mind state. He was being pulled forward and when he thought about Aoife, niggling questions kept coming back. Why had he not been sad when she died? Was he running away from something? He just did not know. He wanted to *feel* more. In some ways he felt weak and vulnerable, very little was straightforward for him and he found relationships complex and scary. Could he trust people? Was the world as messed-up as he believed it to be?

He worked the land like he had as a boy, losing himself in that place, tuning into the nuances of the changing seasons – the gentle rise in spring temperatures, noticing the long held winter mud on the path begin to solidify and set footprints in place, which in turn would change shape, dry up and fade to dust in time. Noticing a thought growing within him, he saw something was solidifying enough so that it could begin to be shaped. It met with resistance from within, a feeling of pointlessness and impossibility. "How could I do that?" he thought "what gives me the right?" He could not decide, could not see a world in which he did what he wanted and stepped out of his normal state of being – hard working, people pleasing, following others' lead - struggling with that and wanting to run away from it all. Where was the inner strength he needed to make choices and feel empowered? He then made a counterintuitive and difficult move and decided to leave his work. He gave six months' notice, enough to finish up the growing season.

There was still no plan but only the feeling of one. He could move to another job in six months or he could make a further choice, which appeared to be there, but had not yet taken shape. It was too big to be allowed space in his mind. He didn't deserve to do it. As summer plants began to grow and bear fruit, the earth warmed and the back of his neck became that leathery brown from hours of stooping at work; planting, hoeing and harvesting under the sun. He realised that to make the choice to do something different he needed help. He saw that his sense of stuckness was often something profound and he felt shame about that, about his lack of motivation. It was as if a huge mountain always lay between him and the fruition of his ideas. The idea that he was a failure was a repeated story he began to hear again, making him realise that he was in fact too much of a failure to do something big for himself. He got help from a life coach who was prepared to work with him even though he paid her far less than her normal rate – she worked with what he could afford. It was a moment of luck and help he needed. He worked with Jana in the following months to create a plan for himself.

Clear Spot

He suddenly felt lucky again, like he was being helped in some way, as if that new feeling had begun to guide him. He was clearing a path through the snaggy undergrowth he had cultivated for decades, ever since he began to think he was not who he was meant to be, when he had first chosen to withdraw.

With the inner quiet he experienced through the plant medicine and the sense of achievement and connection he found through learning to swim and working at the market garden, he began see a way out of his doubt. His coach helped him see his own mental blocks, and that he needn't be afraid of who he was and of his potential. He saw that life had become a serious 'problem' for him, something he had to figure out and try to solve, which made him always want to control situations and outcomes so he wouldn't feel hurt or excluded. Happy go lucky he was not. But he was starting to see beyond that and a plan for something big and bold began to emerge.

Bit by bit the idea of doing a charity walk in memory of his sister started to become real. The idea was easy to dream up, but making the choice to commit to it was difficult as he was so used to remaining at the 'ideas' stage, never braving the actual 'doing' part. He laboured for months over it, finally making the actual decision in November, that he would do the walk the following spring. What a relief! Beth was behind him and he felt so grateful for her support. Their daughter was three years old and it would be hard for Beth but she was completely on board. He began telling his family. The excitement started to build.

Walk For Aoife

He began training for the walk in February, three months before setting off. He had never trained for anything before, apart from when he took up boxing for a while when he was thirteen, in a fantasy of becoming tough and attracting girls. He lasted about six months with the boxing. He asked Harry, the swimming coach and personal trainer, for some help and Harry made a plan for free. He trained without weights or gym to save money, just using his own bodyweight for things like push ups and squats, running and walking – some intense interval training which made him feel like he was going to die through over-exertion. He didn't particularly enjoy the training, but felt it was necessary and knew he needed it in order to be physically strong for the walk. He began to feel fit and bouncy, losing weight, which improved his confidence. He got a part time job in Unicorn, a wholefood shop, part of his local food family. He walked to work and back, a nine-mile round trip. As Manchester's soggy winter turned to spring, he ran in Highfield Park, squelching in the playing field in his less than adequate trainers, jumping and dodging huge, dark brown puddles, which would sit for weeks in the long winter dampness. Highfield Park was a disused claypit and brickworks, then becoming a bleach and dyeworks and later the site of a tripe factory, then a landfill site before finally being turned into a park. He felt for its sad history but he was grateful for that place and for its semi-abandoned state, which meant it was quiet, had many animals and hidden, overgrown parts. He was courted by wrens and chastised by blackbirds as he trained.

He couldn't help but compare the park to where he grew up and thought he could feel the exhausted land heavily bearing its past. In winter, especially, the vegetation died away to reveal years of rubbish, which appeared to grow back out of the land, as if people had lost hope of relationship with nature, easier to continue the pollution than be vulnerable enough to look at the mess. He wondered if his life would continue to change, and whether doing the walk would bring him the perspective he so desperately wanted. He mourned for the effect humans had on the world.

Help

A big part of his journey was the fundraising. He decided that he would try to raise £50k for charity – a huge figure but a motivational 'carrot and stick'. He would raise the money for two charities, one in Manchester and the other in Dingle. Both charities were chosen because they dealt with either mental health or disability. He organised a gig, musicians kindly played for free. Volunteers sold cakes, beer and bric a brac – many people volunteered their time and skills to help. His daughter's nursery school raised around £1000, releasing balloons with messages on them, some of which made it across the Irish Sea. His friend Mike, owner of a specialised drainage technology company, told him he would donate for every manhole cover he photographed and shared on social media. He felt his community and the support of those around him – he was doing something heartfelt that was bringing people together in some way. One generous soul, Gwyn, bought him a waterproof jacket for his journey. He borrowed gear, including a rucksack, tent and camping equipment. He felt the support of many, the pull of the road, and found a satisfied frame of mind within it all. He knew he didn't really know what he was doing, but he was filled with optimism about the journey ahead. He felt he could not fail. Then there was getting help with the next problem – crossing the Irish Sea. Fortunately for him, his friend Eddy was about to surface.

Sea Change

At some point that winter he had decided that catching the ferry the sixty miles across the Irish Sea was a little too conventional for that walk. He asked friends, considered hiring a boat and a rowing crew, catching a lift on a yacht, even crossing by pedal boat. None of those options bore fruit, but a post on an adventure forum Explorers Connect brought Mike Alexander into the frame. Mike, a five star kayaking instructor was willing to accompany him across the sea – from North Wales to Dublin - in a double kayak. Big stuff considering how poorly he swam and the small fact that he'd never been in a sea kayak before.

His first ever sea kayak experience, ten days later, involved a paddle around Aberdovey estuary, in North Wales with Mike. He loved kayaking straight away but felt a rising panic about the controlled capsize that was planned for the end, realising that his recently overcome fear of deep water wasn't as cut and dried as he'd expected. As they tipped the kayak over, he felt shock and panic as his body hit the cold March seawater. The scramble to exit the kayak whilst upside down and underwater, then popping back up to the surface with the help of the buoyancy aid, felt disorienting and disconcerting.

Afterwards they had lunch at a seafront café, and he was still shaken from the capsize experience. There, he began to feel the gravity of the situation. What he was taking on was dawning on him and fear very quickly flooded in. What was he thinking? He could barely even swim! He had made moves to do the craziest thing he had ever attempted in his life and there he was, with a stranger, eating Welsh rarebit for the first time, in Wales, having just stepped so far outside his comfort zone he was practically in space. He could barely speak. They talked about the crossing as if it was actually going to happen. Things got very real for him in that moment.

After the terror in the café he made the choice and, although petrified at some level, he knew that when he had decided, it was a waste of time to worry. He trusted that it would work out and allowed no doubt to cross his mind. There would be some associated costs, which his friend Eddy took care of. This was a powerful contribution and show of support, allowing him to feel confident with the challenge itself and not worried about money, for once.

For the first time in his life, perhaps, he found a resolve that was stronger than he had ever felt and no words of discouragement or concern from others would stop him. He was scared but he was committed. Deep water, sixty miles of open sea – there was plenty to fear. But this time he was actually doing it. He had all sorts of offers of help, people saying they wanted to buy him a ferry ticket or fund the crossing some other way. Some people even told him he wouldn't make it, perhaps to discourage him. All of these reactions he took lightly, they only served to strengthen his newfound drive.

Part Three - The Road Begins

The day he set off was sunny. He said goodbye to his family who had walked the first few miles with him, chasing his daughter along the Fallowfield Loop's tarmacked path – its long grassy borders presenting strong spring growth and excellent dog turd concealment qualities. It was a green corridor through the city's urban blanket, a sunken, displaced winding serpent of spent railway – a great example of urban repurposing. Once they had cleared the Loop they said goodbye in Chorlton with a final, fun chat with some friends outside Steph's café *Love Juice* and he walked steadily on towards the canal.

The feeling of leaving the city knowing he was going home was unique. There was elation, the idea of having planned something that was being carried out – an amazing feat for a man who felt he'd achieved so little in his life. As the buildings became fewer around him, eventually turning to hedgerow, tree and bridge on that hazy sunlit day he was filled with hope and excitement for the journey that lay ahead. The people he would meet and the experiences ahead of him all melted into one exciting prospect, something he had been preparing for all his life – a chance to be alone with his grief and to connect with his lost sister in some way he did not yet understand.

The next day after stopping for lunch and having crossed many stiles and traversed paths on the typically English landscape with its large oak-flecked fields of cows, occasional expansive countryside views and little villages, one of which was hosting a steam engine rally, he began to feel a dull pain on the ball of his right foot. His bag began to feel too heavy and it creaked and heaved with every stile crossing. He stopped at one point to dunk his feet in the canal, feeling the momentary relief it brought. The day was fine and sunny – settled spring weather, which he felt lucky to have. But he was now suffering and struggling with pain. The last miles of that day felt very painful and arduous and a growing sense that there was something wrong began to consume him. Once he got to the campsite at Delamere forest, he was relieved to have completed fifteen miles. When he peeled off his socks the inevitable truth was revealed – he had a huge blister on the ball of each foot. The heavy bag? The shoes? He didn't know what to blame as he hobbled round the campsite on his heels, with stinging foot pain.

The Road Begins

Cooking his dinner he cut himself with the new, sharp knife he'd bought for the trip. Seconds later he burned himself on the stove as it fell apart before his eyes. He laughed out loud at his ineptitude and enjoyed that moment on the grass; free to burn and cut himself and learn how to do things properly. Then he tackled the giant blisters, painfully popping each one using the 'needle and thread' method. It was a hugely stressful operation, not only because of the sheer size of the things, (they were each about an inch in diameter) but he knew he would have to walk on these raw feet every day and there was nothing he could do to change that.

He felt great being outdoors. He revelled in the treeline in front of him and the blackbirds singing their dissonant evening song. He felt comforted within the safety of the trees. He spent some time just staring at that treeline, feeling protected and happy. He had time to stop and feel that sense of achievement at having walked through the pain of the day *and* survived popping the bulbous blisters on the bottom of his feet. As he reflected a light rain began and he gathered all his gear and headed tentwards. He pulled everything inside, zipped up the front, read for a little bit and began to drift off, exhausted. He lay there listening to the raindrops on the tent cover in a half-dream. He felt he could hear each raindrop individually, not as rain but as some kind of cosmic conversation, as if his day of stress and pain had opened up another dimension of experience for him. The raindrops were talking to him. All at different levels and depths. He could hear that their song was full of humour and life.

The next morning he didn't want to get up. He was happy in his cocoon, not facing the pain of putting on his shoes and having to head off into discomfort for what could be days or longer – he had no experience or idea about how long blisters like those would take to heal, especially with walking on them every day. It was too much to think about. So he got up, had his rehydrated porridge in a bag and enjoyed the simplicity and lack of washing up of such a meal. Of course, the amount of plastic discarded after every plastic coated meal kind of dulled that satisfaction. He could however get a sense of expeditions through glaciers, on oceans and hard to reach places, and of how the quick and simple meal could make the whole journey less hassle. He wondered if he would ever go on such a journey and his imagination went that way for a little while. It was cool and fresh that morning and the damp grass of the campsite soothed the hot soles of his feet. He lingered there on the grass, which helped prepare him for the day.

That day was an easy walk. He met an old friend and they walked together seven to his house – only seven miles from Delamere forest. He was so well looked after by Ged and his family and as they spent time together in the garden, he forgot about blisters and focussed on catching up and feeling support. He could also gauge their reaction to the blisters when he showed them – he could see in their faces they were visibly shocked and this in turn shocked him. He knew he must continue, at least for as long as he could. His thoughts were harassing him, telling him he'd already failed, that he wouldn't make it to the next place. How could he have messed up so badly?

Leaving England – The Longest Day

As he headed towards Chester it was morning rush hour. Cars, trucks and buses, slowly rolled by and he reminded himself how lucky he was to be doing the journey. He also felt like a bit of an eccentric and out of place on that busy, straight road he was plodding, with his massive, creaking rucksack. Everyone on their way to work, looking at him from inside their cars and trucks. Although he was the one everyone could see he felt like the voyeur. He was having an insight into the lives of thousands of people as he walked along that long road into Chester. It felt alien to him seeing those people sitting in their cars, driving slowly for a few miles then going into their jobs. He wondered what they thought when they saw him, walking and occasionally randomly photographing manhole covers.

He wasn't on a busy, daily commute, but was walking a path nobody had ever walked before. As he made his way against the creeping flow of traffic, he realised the uniqueness of his journey. He was walking a route designed by him, for his story and circumstances. It was his and no matter how crazy he may have looked or felt in that moment he knew the power he was carrying inside. He had a mission to do things he had never done, to step out of the world that had held him for so long and into the wilds of unknown possibility. Each day he was encountering the unfamiliar and new and he had the privilege of just passing through and gaining a glimpse of these places and people.

In his quieter moments he would worry about what he was doing and where the journey was taking him in terms of his capability. He was already beginning to feel like a failure. There was an amount of self-pity going on and the classic mantra of "I'm doing it wrong" crept in. He went into a loop, cursing himself for the stupidity of not training enough. Was he wearing the wrong shoes? Did he not walk far enough in his training? He had been very concerned about footwear. Was he worrying about it too much? Was there a point to him even continuing?

He walked through fields of long grass, ready for silage, the sward flaying his bare legs. He negotiated ditches and stiles, often the path was not obvious and hadn't been walked for some time, which was the cause of stress and with the state his feet were in, every wrong turn felt costly. What looked at the planning stage like sensible shortcuts were in reality niggling, labyrinthine puzzles. When after about an hour of walking round a series of fields he could see no sign of the exit, he began to feel stressed. His legs were a bumpy red mass of nettle stings and grass welts. He was lost, trying to find his way on a path that didn't exist when literally just yards away the discomforting sound of rattling trucks speeding by on the A55 expressway, filled his ears.

He was penned in, a creature wandering around the borders of fields into trees. Unsure of the terrain underfoot because of long grass and nettles, he nervously picked his way, lifting legs like a deerstalker trying to avoid detection, but feeling more like a lost idiot in a field. His arms and shoulders were in pain, ready to drop the bag and find a way to end the torturous walk. It did not take much for him to go into a spiral of failure and negative thoughts. "How could I do this to myself?" "This walk is such a stupid idea, how could I be so stupid and unprepared?" he questioned repeatedly. He felt weak and tired and in pain. It all felt wrong. He was failing miserably.

He had made the first few days of his route at home on his computer, based on Ordnance Survey maps, but unwittingly using trails that were long overgrown and underused; looking at the route from the bird's' eye view of an OS drawing was all very well, where he observed plenty 'official' trails and paths through fields and over hills, which he thought were 'safe'. They were safe (when they were visible) but in truth, he had no idea what was actually there when he planned the route, and there he was putting himself in a bad situation. Already 'injured', (his poor feet were throbbing after the effort) and wandering through what seemed like an endless number of fields, trees and stiles, each a new terrain, needing a new assessment and attitude in order to get through. It was taking forever! It was a BIG journey. He knew he would have to change something in order to keep going as he was feeling that he was getting nowhere. He didn't dare look at the rest of the route on his GPS, fearing how far it was. He was, it's fair to say, having a somewhat difficult morning.

When he finally found the stile to take him across the A55 there was a little sign that read 'PATH CLOSED -

NO ALTERNATIVE ROUTE'. The only answer was to retrace his steps for an hour and divert from further back. The sign mentioned something about works on the railway. There was no way he was turning back. Directly in front of him were the A55 expressway and the railway tracks, running parallel - both needed to be crossed, for a start. He picked his way across the busy dual carriageway and the train tracks were fenced off, with signs warning him away. He walked alongside until he found a spot where he could jump the fence and was away. He was then back in more fields with long grass, cows and the occasional dead tree along the fence line. The immensity of the walk was hitting him again. There he was, probably only halfway through his day and already tired and feeling lost. The tracks, stiles and diversions were taking their toll, with the heavy rucksack and bad feet. Each wooden stile needed extra effort to negotiate, especially the overgrown or rotting ones.

He flicked through the audiobooks on his mp3 player, settling on Victor Frankl's 'Man's Search for Meaning.' This put things in some perspective for him. He was able to see his pain and suffering for what it really was in those moments – something he had - in some sense – chosen to undergo. The realization that he had been free to make that choice, along with the relatively little amount of short term physical suffering he was going through compared to people in Nazi concentration camps, gave him perspective. His clouds lifted for a while and he learned to enjoy the fields of long grass and nettles, being surrounded by beautiful nature, good weather and the freedom of the walk. The pain was almost inconsequential and he felt grateful that he had more food in his bag than he could eat. The stories in the book relating to food and how people were slowly and intentionally starved to death in the concentration camps struck deep. He felt grateful for living in a world where he had an unlimited amount of food available to him. He had the choice to stop, go home and rest at any time and whatever he did was his own choice. *That* was what one form of liberation felt like. And although he came in and out of those thoughts and ideas in those days, the fact that he had experienced 'Man's Search for Meaning' was definitely a perspective giver and helped him to feel so absolutely privileged for the whole opportunity of the walk, which he had created for himself. One of the key messages of the book was something he would come back to many times during the following weeks – the idea that people choose what they allow into their lives to affect them. Frankl describes in the book how some people, despite the harshest and cruellest of conditions seemed to maintain some kind of happy state – or at least were able to detach from the horror of what was happening and survive without going crazy – and this is what fascinated him. That somewhere within every person there is the potential of resilience to handle any situation. For Frankl it was finding meaning within his life, which helped him connect with that resilience.

Bullhonky

One field was full of Jersey cows. And a bull. He knew it was a bad idea to be anywhere near a bull, as back home they were generally known to be pretty dangerous. Jerseys, he knew, had a friendly nature, but he had never met a Jersey bull before. He was big! He stuck to the hedge, walking the perimeter. The bull spotted him and started moving. The whole herd followed. He quickened his pace, heading toward the crossing point at the opposite fence. No sign of it. He broke into a run. His rucksack, a dead weight on his back, working solidly against him, dragged him down with each step. The whole herd, led by the bull was thundering towards him, about 20 metres behind. There was a sheep wire fence ahead with barbed wire on top. He went for it, grabbing the barbed wire in his hand and pushing it down so it met the top of the sheep wire and held them together while he put one foot in and threw the other over. He wobbled and lurched on top for a moment with his massive bag and then pulled the other leg over. He was inches away from the whole herd, which had suddenly stopped and was observing him in a friendly and inquisitive manner from the other side of the fence. Even the bull, close up, could have been his chum. He looked lovely. They were probably just joining in with his game of 'running across the field', anything to break the monotony of field life. He laughed aloud at the absurdity of it all and was annoyed at the same time. "Stupid fence, stupid me!" Wandering around fields and nettles. Pulsing, painful feet, ridiculously heavy bag!

He met many cows and cattle on those first few days and wondered if he would meet any people. He felt increasingly sorry for those docile animals - grazing away in slavery. He supposed their lives weren't too bad, but he wished for a revolution within their ranks, which would take them up over the fence and on to some wild pasture somewhere so they could live a peaceful, happy life. He felt sorry for the whole species, which humans breed, eat and do whatever they want with. They were living animals after all with personalities, individuality and culture and people looked at them like they were cash and food. He grew up with cows and never really felt any love for them, regarding them in that same way. He wasn't interested in the animal side of farming; he felt most at home behind the wheel of a tractor or doing some kind of physical work. He just didn't feel the connection with the cows. Until those moments on his walk.

There wasn't a feeling of love for the animals back home. Dogs and cats lived outdoors and their job was clear, they were working animals, dogs for herding or security, and cats were mousers and ratters. Cattle and sheep brought in the money and were a source of food, but he never heard talk of the animals outside of their functionality. They used to slaughter their own animals for food each year. The relationship was practical, perhaps even cold, to him - there was a good distance between them and their beasts, despite the fact that it had been commonplace for animals to live in houses with their people only a hundred years before. Had they cut themselves off from connection with these animals, just as humans in general had cut themselves off from the land?

Cows were a commodity, this being a symptom perhaps of the ease with which people can grow a protein-rich food and that relationship is, sadly both destructive to the environment and disconnected from the animals themselves. Cows, like the oceans, forests and thousands of species humans slowly eradicate – are not going to complain at being mistreated. The Earth doesn't say "OK, hang on, guys. You're kinda making a massive mess of things now and I will start killing hundreds of thousands of you every day until you change your ways." If only it were that simple and humans could reconnect with nature in a new way, in a healing way rather than a destructive, abusive way. That feeling he had was guilt and as he stared at the stupid cows he began to see it was he that was stupid, for feeling resentful of those docile beasts, for being a person who all his life had been docile himself, too afraid to get involved in the messiness of the world, he'd rather just observe from afar. Humans had a choice, just like Victor Frankl wrote. To do nothing and feel awful or become OK with what was going on and act from that standpoint.

He made lunch under a shady oak in a field of young wheat. A path of yellow, 'dead wheat' had been burned right through the centre of this field with roundup. He thought twice about even being in the field, which had been so obviously poisoned but it seemed like the best place to stop. He felt for the plants, soil and creatures, which had been poisoned, whilst being a bit concerned for his safety. He knew that roundup stays in the soil for a long time after application, but he was weary enough to get the stove and food out all the same. He decided not to remove the shoes at break time, partly because he was afraid to witness the state of his feet and partly because he wanted to get used to going all day without needing to inspect 'the damage'.

On he went into the heat. There was a good-looking country pub full of what looked like office workers enjoying the fine weather, chattering away on the outside patio. He didn't allow himself to stop for a drink, although it would certainly have been lovely. He was on a mission and was perhaps too hard on himself to stop. Moments later he crossed the border into Wales.

What a feeling to actually have walked to Wales! Still, he acknowledged with a laugh that he was only about a one-hour drive from his house. The intense experiences he had had these past days through slowing down were an eye opener. He was actually getting somewhere. Psychologically, however, the walk had come to a halt as soon as he got the blisters so close to home. He realised that he had left part of his consciousness back there and was living in the pain and disappointment that he may not be able to continue and was already feeling like a failure. This held him back, created a space, which hindered progress and took him away from the present moment. Still, he was amazed he had made it to Wales.

He had come through what felt like the first part of his journey. He had walked from one country to another and was fine, although still full of doubt and uncertainty and pain. The pain in his feet was more than just blisters. All his life he had decided that he did not want to face the pain, so he had always chosen to run away – into his thoughts and worries, alcohol, highs, porn, smoking and work. There had always been something better to do than experience his own pain. Now he could not escape – he had put the journey in front of himself and pulling out was almost too difficult to imagine – after all his planning and sharing on social media – all this was helping drive him on.

Wales felt welcoming. The farms went from the massive Cheshire plains with giant fields, farm machinery and wildlife deficit to more modest fields with more hedgerows and slightly unkempt machinery - an altogether more rustic scene. Rusting corrugated iron sheds held ancient tractors and implements – the feeling was of a certain amount of making do and scraping a living, which was what he had grown up with and was still doing himself, in many ways. It was familiar and comforting. He felt unleashed again. He had chosen to walk over roads and tracks. Every wooden, nettle filled stile presented its own obstacle – a choice. He chose to slow down and pace himself. He chose to have a short break every two hours.

The Other Uncle and a Path to Inner Nature

When he first arrived in England at 19 years of age, he didn't know that he would not return home, his intention was to go for a summer. He went with a friend, Tim, who he got on well with. Soon after, they struggled with communication, Tim left and headed back home to study. He remained and became lost in the city, getting drunk and taking drugs. He forgot about home and his family, went through a series of jobs, packing satellite receiver fascias into plastic bags at McKechnie Plastic Components, packing production line meals into plastic containers, packing dishes into a washer in a Hotel kitchen. Still, he felt free and rebellious, answering to no-one, with no thought for tomorrow, for his own feelings or the feelings of those he left behind. He was so relieved to go that he became lost in the lie that his past didn't exist, having bombs of amphetamine for breakfast, losing jobs, living with heroin users and criminals.

Unaware, he was suddenly in a situation where he was out of work and squatting in his friend's rented house with no thought for his situation, no job and no hope or idea of what could change for him, all within three months of arriving in England. It did not occur to him that he was on the edge, vulnerable and near destitution. He just wanted to withdraw, relieved that he was no longer in the situation he grew up in, wanting escape from his feelings. Then family reached out. His uncle Jim, who lived near Manchester, happened to phone the house the day the bill was paid and the phone reconnected, telling him there was a job for him if he wanted it. He took that opportunity, having nothing else and was picked up by his uncle and driven to Oldham where he began the next phase of his life.

His uncle Jim became one of the most influential figures in his life and he lodged with him for three years. He was sorted out with a job as a gardener with Rochdale Council, which was perfect for him and his uncle helped ground him and expanded his mind through great writers such as Joyce and Dostoyevsky. He was opened up to the world of his mind and soul through reading psychology books and Carl Jung.

It could have gone the other way just as easily.

He made friends there, taught himself the drums and got his first kit. He started jamming with friends and getting into bands. He was in a supportive place to rest and recover, in some way. Some of the people there became his surrogate family and he felt supported and loved by them. It was unexpected and welcome. His uncle was a community figure there and had done many great things to bring people together. He was a role model for him in terms of community development and cohesion, for being open, welcoming and trusting, regardless of the cost.

Slowly it began to dawn on him that somewhere within he was not lost, that a deeper knowing lay within him, a quiet part, beyond his own personal feelings. It was a spiritual awakening of sorts, shedding light on a world he had never thought possible, but could identify with. A world of symbolic language and metaphor, of poetry and meaning and he felt that his uncle helped him reach a part of himself that nobody could see – a freedom within that was possible, a connection to the unknown, to 'home'. An unnameable feeling he carried within him was being touched and he felt himself opening up to some kind of truth in a way he never before had. This lasted for the years he lived with his uncle, but when he finally moved out and into the world a bit more, that connection soon faded and he then only wondered about its existence, couldn't work out how to reconnect with it and slowly he let it go altogether, settling back into his old patterns of fear and mistrust. But he'd had a glimpse of freedom and he carried that within.

Struggle and Support

Living day to day, with the purpose of healing and adventure, of connecting with the past and all he had run away from, was where his journey had brought him, twenty years on. As his uncle had said to him many times, he was 'being looked after' and he knew it, despite the negative slant he was often able to bring to it, feeling unable to look after himself, failing to be strong like others who choose a path to some kind of worldly success. He had hit rock bottom without knowing it and had to be taken care of. He had no idea what it took for his uncle to take him in - a troubled, depressed teenager. He wondered if he would ever find a way to be satisfied with his achievements, and if he could work with that part of him whose voice was so loud, often he could hear little else. The dark side, or The Shadow, as Jung called it.

By the time he walked to the outskirts of Mold in North Wales, he was struggling; feeling like he had walked too far that day. He stopped for an ice cream at a garage. It was delicious! He sat on a bridge with the water flowing underneath, cooling his thoughts and imagined putting his feet in there, feeling the water running over them. He had made a pact with himself to not remove the shoes until he got to his friend James' house. On he went, struggling up the hill and got to James' front door. He had left the keys outside, under a flowerpot. He went in the front door and then straight out the back door to take his shoes and socks off. He had been walking for eight hours, covering 15 miles, less than two miles per hour.

He carefully peeled off each sock and they stuck where the blister plasters were. The plasters had partly disintegrated where he had been walking on them all day and they were welded to his wool socks. He carefully peeled them off and then peeled the plaster membrane slowly away from his skin, which was tattered and white. The flesh underneath was an angry red. Both feet were swollen and were now screaming their protest at having been walked on all day. He sat down, but couldn't get comfortable. His feet were stinging harshly, disturbing his rest.

He got in the shower, the foot pain and sore shoulders from the heavy rucksack distracted him from what could have been a blissful moment. A couple of painkillers later he sat in the kitchen and wrote a less than positive journal entry about his day. He was angry with himself. The throbbing pain in his feet meant he could not get comfortable. They were not happy. He didn't think he had done too badly, considering the discomfort, but the inner voice told him he should be ashamed.

James came home and they chatted. It was great to see him and have the distraction from the pulsing feet. He sat in the kitchen while James made dinner. After a while he became overwhelmed with the pain and went to lie down with his feet raised for a bit. He put his feet up on the arm of the couch and read a little. He was still very distracted and had to then lie on his back and put his feet in the air. This felt marginally less painful so he stayed in that position until dinnertime. James came and checked every now and again and listened to his complaints. "I think it's more serious," he said. "I might need to go to the hospital". James just nodded in a supportive way and thankfully stayed completely out of his worries. He was concerned that he had hurt himself too much. The pain was trying to tell him something - that he should rest for a day or should be looking after himself better. He was genuinely worried about continuing the journey. He was in a lot of pain and the weather forecast said heavy rain the next day.

He was beginning to convince himself that the worst was occurring. He was afraid to continue and it was no surprise - the reward would be a lot more pain than he was comfortable with. He could feel the self-pity of old creeping in and began to feel trapped by his emotions. "This is terrible. I am really going to have to suffer to make this happen. It shouldn't be like this. It's not fair." Six hours after reaching James' house, the painful throbbing began to subside, in time for sleep. His mind then also calmed enough so he drifted off and slept the whole night comfortably.

Spits and Spots

In the morning they had breakfast and were ready to head off. He was still a bit shaky and, looking at the forecast expressed his apprehension to James about crossing the Clwydian hills to Denbigh. Heavy rain was still forecast and as they set off, he was amazed at James' optimism about the weather. James wore a light pair of plimsoll-style shoes and a jacket that did not even look waterproof. He wondered why James would head out on a hike up a 300 metre hill so unprepared and felt a bit uneasy about the day ahead. When he reminded James of the rain that was forecast he just said in his relaxed Donegal way "Agh, spits and spots!" James' confidence led him on, but he definitely did not feel comfortable nor confident about it himself. James offered to share the burden of the giant rucksack. He agreed to share, but went first.

They went through woods and then the beautiful Loggerheads Park. The conversation flowed and the bag sharing truly was a revelation; they were up to the top in no time, marvelling at the view and without any rain. They were joking and giggling about the surreal nature of the situation; walking all these miles and everything associated with it, when out of nowhere a man suddenly walked straight up to them, demanding "Where's your dog?!" Taken aback, they looked at each other knowing they had no dog but this man was convinced he had seen him (a walker) with some kind of terrier a bit further along. The confused questioner stomped on, leading James to the story that he was 'the walker' and in a parallel universe James was *his* dog, running alongside him and yapping away excitedly as they walked through the hills. It made them laugh and it sort of fitted too, in some way. Then he took a selfie of the two of them on the hill and, on closer inspection, the man who had approached them was also in the photo, walking along the peak of James' hat, like a tiny elf. This was the icing on the cake and helped them feel like all was not as it appeared to be – that there was some kind of magical fun available through conversation and shifts in perspective in the moment. This led from one reality-bending conversation to another.

The Road Begins

They walked the ridge of the hills, which was also the Offa's Dyke path, for the next few miles. There was the beginning of some rain that never really materialised when they met a man who was walking Offa's Dyke for charity and was on his final day. "The blisters are bad this time", said the man, who was around 70. He winced on hearing this, imagining himself at that age, doing charity walks and still getting blisters. He shook that off and they walked on. They sat and ate leftover curry on a bench on the hillside at a pass, then took the road downwards in the direction of Denbigh.

He talked to James about Aoife on the final part of that day. He told James how he felt about her life and what he thought he was carrying around with him. He forced himself to do it because it was weighing him down. Part of the journey was about healing for him, he felt strongly that he needed to talk and gain some perspective. It felt good to just say what was on his mind about Aoife and although he didn't feel any dramatic difference after he'd said it, this was him getting used to talking about his sister to people who didn't know her or him growing up in Ireland.

He wanted Aoife with him on the walk, even if it was to connect him with a higher purpose within the walk, a reason to keep going, always. He felt that this was his lot and that perhaps he could accept it, despite the pain. He had trained and prepared himself for the journey, and it definitely was not going to plan. This was what he got. He had to trust that if Aoife was OK with it, then so was he. He felt that somehow she was 'around', influencing events, helping him to feel pain and get through it, rather than his usual trick of getting scared and running away. He was experiencing his amazing sister in a similar way to how he experienced his other amazing sisters – as a supportive friend, like James had been for him, on the darkest day of his walk so far. It was something he hadn't seen before, because it felt foolish to think that Aoife, who needed help with everything all her life, could ever be there for him. It meant something to him to view things that way.

The previous day had been difficult and dark, but having James there helped him see that, despite the journey being a solo one, friends were there to help, to distract, to listen to complaints and fears. He could see that people were there for him despite his feeling that he should be managing it all by himself. Also, that one man's heavy rain was another's spits and spots – perspective and outlook had a part to play. They arrived at Rachel and Bryn's house for about 3pm, a bit weary, but after a very satisfying walk. James had delivered him safely, they hugged and he headed off to work his nightshift.

Being at his old friends' house was like being at home and he was supremely well looked after and glad to be there. Their house was his base for the following 2 days' hike and they did everything to help make those days both easy and enjoyable.

When he saw the lengths people were going to in order to help he was definitely seeing a pattern. These were people he knew, granted, but it felt like a step up from what he usually experienced. He saw himself on this idiosyncratic journey, sometimes as a kind of crazy man, 'the walker' with his yapping mind; a guy walking a crazy journey alone, driven by emotions and the need to figure out parts of his life. Walking an unestablished route, door to door; through so many doors he thought he would never open. When he actually caught himself thinking about what he was doing he felt a bit crazy and began questioning himself. "What are you doing? I mean what are you *actually* doing here? Dreaming up this whole campaign where you're planning to raise loads of money. Writing and seeking out media attention? Who do you think you are?" Then the negative voice of "How could you be so selfish, putting people out, dragging everyone into your wacky dream. Think about your poor wife and child; Beth must be finding it really difficult with you away and here you are 'on holiday' being treated like a king everywhere you go while she's at home struggling to keep everything afloat. You're not even in a permanent job so there's no paid holiday for you for 6 weeks. And what are you going to do when you get back? Part-time work? You quit your secure job - minimum wage was better than no wage. What are you going to do?"

The Only Way Out is Through

The following day he and Bryn (and Tecs the lurcher) walked twenty miles through the beautiful North Wales countryside, the undulating landscape informing their varying conversation. At one point he spotted a tawny owl dead at the side of the road. It was a sad sight. It had been freshly killed, perhaps hit by a car or truck, its body still warm and limp. He looked into its shiny dark eyes and in that moment felt compelled to take a feather from its wing. This was an unusual thing for him to do but he trusted it and felt that the bird, although dead, was some kind of positive sign. He took the feather and a moment to thank the bird for what he took to be a sign of safe passage across the sea.

That evening they laughed, chatted and ate good food, he felt the support of others and the specialness of what he was doing. It was reassuring, especially with the physical suffering he'd had, the past two days' company had made a big difference to his state of mind and feeling of achievement. He needed others to tell him he was doing well, because when he looked at it, the journey was feeling like somewhat of a failure to him – that inner voice, coupled with the physical pain he felt, was the perfect recipe for the failure mind set.

The pain in his feet was still very strong and in his quiet moments he struggled and suffered – both with the injury and with his idea of what it meant. He felt lucky to have such great support, but also worried that he would let them down through not being able to finish. Another reason to feel bad and unworthy. The pain in his feet and the contrasting kindness he was being shown were parts of a confusing recipe for him as he was so used to suffering alone, to not sharing his pain with anyone, apart from Beth who was always there for him, always having time for his complaints and insecurities. But this time the personal issues were physical, visible, as if they were a manifestation of what he went through in his mind, and he had to accept help to feel better.

The Road Begins

Everything should have been straightforward as he progressed, but he was struggling and fear was beginning to take hold. He felt the pressure of the fundraising, to put on a brave face and smile through the pain. He also didn't want to let his supporters down – those people who looked after him. The uncertain miles ahead also concerned him, as he was without much of a plan for accommodation or support beyond that point. As he walked the last few miles with Bryn he shared the insecurity and unworthiness he felt, uncertain of whether people really cared for him or whether they just felt sorry for him and felt obliged to help. This path of low self-esteem always led him to a dark place, the feeling that he was 'crazy' and the idea that people felt sorry for him was something he had carried with him since childhood. It was self-indulgent and self-conscious, but not self-aware.

When they hit the coastal path in North Wales the next day it was stunning. He had driven the route many times, but now on this perfectly sunny spring day, it felt Mediterranean. Knowing he'd come this far on foot was comforting. He felt fitter and faster. His feet were beginning to feel a bit better and it felt like he and Bryn glided through the rocky headlands, the Irish Sea glistening invitingly. He then realised that his journey thus far had been a journey towards the coast, towards the kayaking challenge that lay ahead. It felt important to be there – to finally see the sea.

The conditions needed to be calm for the kayaking part. He expected to have to wait several days for the appropriate weather to arrive. It was looking good, having had a long spell of warm, settled weather so far, and the forecast for the following days was promising. His arrival at the coast and the first glimpses of the Irish Sea made him feel committed, but he was also aware of a niggling superstition, as if he was looking for more signs of safe passage, or omens for that part of the journey. So far the weather had been good, but his injuries had slowed him down and gave him much unexpected pain and suffering, and that made him curious about the challenges the kayaking would bring.

Bloated Toad

He and Bryn were heading round a bend right on the sea when he spotted an almost dead, bloated toad right next to the path. The poor thing had perhaps lost its way and was dying in the heat. When he saw it a shockwave of worry washed over him. He began seeing this as a negative omen for the kayaking journey, the previous day's owl somehow negated by the toad. He spent the next half hour worrying intensely about this apparition and eventually, to break the spell he told Bryn about it. This wasn't something he was used to doing and he was a bit sheepish as he imparted the story. The idea of creating meaning from the world around him was important, but his pattern was often to create inexplicable and worrying meaning.

Relating that story to Bryn he could see where it took him, into his own depths, where he needed to be, in some way. He had to experience that level of feeling low, the fear and fringes of paranoia. Just like when he was a child, he hid it from almost everyone, never asked for help and 'managed' it all alone. A bit like when he'd had a bad acid trip one time, when he was about twenty, which left him with a sense of paranoia that lasted for years. At the time, he saw his paranoia as insight, but it became torturous. It made him more sensitive to people, to 'signs' that something was wrong. He made up a whole world of 'wrong' for himself, where different signs would appear and bring meaning, a world nobody else could relate to or understand. This lasted for a few years until he talked himself out of it through using affirmations and therapy. He was ashamed that it had happened, that he had let it happen. It had been another way for him to feel weak. And yes he did recover, but he had put up more walls to protect himself. In some ways he hid deeper, pretended to be OK, but really he came across as unbalanced and wouldn't let anyone in. People couldn't figure him out and that's how he liked it. His inner world was often complex and impenetrable, in his twenties. That toad had brought him back in touch with that meaning-making feeling and how it used to unbalance him - seeing a positive sign and then a negative one. Allowing thoughts to sit in his mind and fester.

After telling Bryn he felt lighter – the story had less power over him. Perhaps what he did not see was the insight from his 'bad trip' – it was there to teach him something. It was a reflection of his state of mind as it was and in fact the paranoia and fear merely showed him what he needed to work with, which he began to see all those years later. At the time he only saw the world through his own self-pity, and the fallout from the acid trip became a foundation for *that* reality instead.

He began talking about Aoife again. He was feeling a little bitter and shared his thoughts with Bryn about how he felt his sister wasn't accepted within the family, and how much pain he had kept inside about her life. He realised as he was talking that the truth of his story was becoming a little thin. He wasn't convincing himself of the long-held beliefs he had about her and his family.

When he talked about Aoife, people would listen quietly and non-judgmentally. He wasn't getting much feedback, which made him feel a little nervous, but he didn't need feedback. Hearing the sound of his own voice echoing out loud and the stories, which had been bouncing around inside for so long, he realised that he wasn't convincing himself of these truths any more. His ideas of unfairness and injustice on his sister's part were beginning to become just stories, as if he had made them up. This was important, he was realising. The great sadness he was holding on to was softening a little, and the resistance he would usually have to telling it, less absorbing. As they walked and he looked out across the sparkling Irish Sea he felt a little of his story evaporate away on that sunny Welsh afternoon.

He left Bryn on the seafront at Llanfairfechan. He wrestled the rucksack back on, and feeling instantly lost and vulnerable again, he hesitantly made his way along the coastal path. After three days of company he was not quite ready to be alone again. A pattern was emerging. When he was with others he felt strong and supported. On his own he often felt weak and desperate, despite thinking that he was independent.

He resisted help from others. He wondered why this was and why he couldn't seem to hold himself together when alone. He felt somewhat pathetic.

The aim was Bangor, about nine miles ahead, still a fair hike. The coastal path became more uncertain and he ended up going off route pretty soon after leaving Bryn. The path ahead, being obvious for the past three days, suddenly became uncertain and quickly he was lost, his feet began to hurt and the worry set in. He had a map but the path didn't seem to be on it. Way off track, he felt like every wrong turn was costing him. He met a walker who helped him back on the route and they walked and chatted for about an hour. She was called Jo and he was grateful to have met her. It was the first conversation he'd had with a stranger about his walk. Jo even offered to give him a lift into Bangor if he didn't feel like walking the whole way. He said he would be fine but she gave him her phone number just in case.

When they parted he was still about five miles from Bangor and feeling it. It was turning into a beautiful evening and he was enjoying every bit of the coastline. Annoyed at himself for not having enough water, he was unable to pitch his tent along that stunning path. His only option was to trudge on into Bangor. He had nowhere to stay that night so he put a social media post out there and a friend generously booked him into a hotel for the night, with the intriguing footnote "I hope it's not a fleapit." Help was all around him and despite feeling like he was neglecting the beauty of that place, he was grateful for how little time it took to find help.

He found a new resolve, had cracked another twenty-mile day and with only about a mile to go, imagined himself triumphantly walking to the door of the hotel and how great that would feel. Then he saw someone waving at him from a bus stop. It was Jo, waiting to give him a lift into Bangor! Taking a lift meant he would have to return to the point he was picked up from, to begin the next day's walk, in order to keep the integrity of walking all the way. He explained his dilemma to her, how he was appreciative of the lift but didn't actually want it, but she was so charming and persuasive that he couldn't refuse. "Come on, jump in!" she said. "You can get the bus back out to here in the morning." To have Jo's support felt great and as they pulled up at the hotel they looked at each other in a puzzled way and she said in a slightly concerned tone "Oh dear, it looks derelict." He laughed because, although it wasn't derelict, it did look as much. They said goodbye and he ventured in.

He stood in the narrow hallway, which had barely enough room for two people, with doors left and right. A balding man was watching a portable TV set with his back to him. He delivered the customary "A-hem" and the man belatedly turned round and with just a hint of resentment looked him up and down, saying, "You're the guy who's walked from Manchester." "That's me!" he replied enthusiastically, with a massive rucksack on his back, feeling somewhat proud yet probably looking desperate and broken. "I'll tell you what mate", he went on, handing over the keys, "you're off your head!" He looked at him in silence for a second, crestfallen. "I've only done a quarter of my journey", he thought.

The Road Begins

He decided not to tell him, thanked him then bungled his way through the right hand door towards his room.

The next two days saw him make his way from Bangor across the beautiful Island of Anglesey, which held many memories for him as a place he travelled to from Manchester to go to the beach, the lighthouse keeper's cottage at Penmon Point he and Beth had stayed at many times and the general feeling of being away from it all in a beautiful, clean coastal place. Crossing the Menai Bridge, he was blown away by the stunning beauty of the Menai Straits one hundred feet below him. It had the appearance of a great river, such as the Potomac in Virginia, where he had once visited with his sister Susan. He wondered about what it was that made a scene so visually striking, to literally stop him in his path to take it in. The power of a place to hold attention, to snap him out of his musings or worry, felt both mysterious and warming.

The weather was perfect; sunny and bright and despite the constant blister pain nagging at him, he felt excited to be crossing the island. The gorse had flowered, adorned with its beautiful, bright yellow beads, while the pain in his feet blossomed once again. Frustrated and angry, he took to singing to help deal with the pain. Walking along the A5, he sang his little heart out. The cows would slowly turn their heads as he passed, casually chewing, taking a moment to check whether the singing lunatic was a threat. He was beyond caring what passing motorists thought. He had always been worried about what others thought, making him hold himself in a tight way. Better to be safe than vulnerable, was his mantra. Now he was making a crazy, public journey and fundraising – he was challenging many of his fears and beginning to feel stronger for it.

That evening Beth and his daughter caught up with him and they spent the night together in a friend's caravan. He was delighted to see his family, he had been through so much, it was difficult for him to describe and he became despondent after a time. He was in the middle of something that had to do with being on his own and he was keen to get going again. He felt some guilt for his feelings, but at the same time he realised he had a strong focus on the journey ahead, which was becoming his purpose in life, even if just for a short time. That evening he sat there resting his feet, feeling a bit useless, listening to the wind whip and whistle around the caravan, wondering if the conditions would be suitable for the kayaking trip he would begin 30 hours later. He left all his camping gear with Beth as a way to save weight – it was time to let some stuff go. The gear was taken back to Manchester, sealing the fate of the rest of the walk's accommodation, as yet unknown. All that mattered to him was what was coming next – sixty miles of open water.

Part Four – The Unknown Universe

Anglesey quickly flowed by as the paddle across the sea occupied his mind. Before he knew it he was walking a single-track lane towards Anglesey Outdoors, where he would meet his kayaking 'captain', Mike. He stopped to watch a horse and foal in a hillocky field, typical of the area, with rocky outcrops and more flowering gorse (or furze bush, as they called it back home). Happy to have what felt like some time on his hands, he walked slowly along. A message from Mike told him the conditions for kayaking would be good the next day. That lazy feeling soon turned into a solid knot in his stomach. At the same time he marvelled at the good fortune of having no delay at that part. It was certainly unusual to have weather that fine. No rain at all during the walk so far, besides the magic rain on that second night in the tent, some spits and spots and a completely smooth transition to the kayaking challenge. He wondered about Aoife and whether she had anything to do with it. Was he being looked after in some way? It sounded ridiculous to him to even think that, but somewhere deep within he was considering this walk to be more than a simple journey – he began the walk with questions and an open mind, rather than the desire to travel and see somewhere. Where would it take him, within? Because he didn't ever know Aoife, he wondered what she might have been capable of. He wanted to approach the idea of his sister with a child-like attitude of possibility and even magic. Because her physical life had been so small, the leap into her being fairy-like and magical was easier for him to consider. Why not? He had nothing to lose. What was 'being dead' anyway? Her life was so restrained, surely now some part of her was flying freely.

Anglesey Outdoors felt like a great, empty alpine style hostel tucked away between rocky hillocks, barely noticeable from the road. He checked in, in the mid-afternoon lull and settled himself in the twin room he and Mike would share. There was an older man running the place and they started talking. The man noticed a lack of kayak and asked about his journey. "I'm doing a walk in memory of my sister who died" he said. "Tomorrow I'm going to kayak across the Irish Sea and then walk another two hundred miles to where I grew up." He was sounding almost blazé about it now, after what he felt he'd come through already. The old man almost immediately went into a story about losing a friend who was fishing off the rocks on Holy Island and how he and some friends organised a rowing trip back and forth from Holyhead to Dublin without touching land to raise money for safety buoys to be installed along the rocks on Holyhead to prevent further tragedies. They worked in teams to row back and forth across the sea and raised the necessary funds. It was a beautiful story and the old man became emotional as he spoke. Both shared a connection between the power of remembrance and marking that with a symbolic journey. After all that, the authorities then wanted to take down the life rings as they hadn't been officially sanctioned. They battled to keep the rings in place and won, thankfully. It was a moment of connection between two men, an acknowledgement of the need for physical challenge to deal with grief and find a way through, to not forget that person and mark their passing in some way. They both felt the connection and lingered there, without a word, in the quiet wood-lined corridor, whose walls were covered in maps and maritime memorabilia. There was a feeling between them he could not define – some kind of deep stirring, that made him feel uncomfortable, unsettled, yet it felt very human and connecting. They bade each other farewell and he wandered off, feeling a little lost.

Mike arrived a couple of hours later with a kayak strapped to his roof and their fate was sealed. That evening they had dinner at the Paddler's Return, the on site bar, and while Mike chatted to fellow paddlers, he stood, lemon-like on the fringes, afraid to even talk about the journey they were going to do. He didn't feel sociable. He wanted to hide. Afterwards they sorted all the gear and prepared for the morning. Mike told him they would stop for five minutes out of every hour to eat and pee and estimated their crossing time at twenty hours. They would launch at ten in the morning on the ebbing tide. The plan was for Mike to get the ferry back from Dun Laoghaire with the kayak, once they had completed their mission, had a rest and a couple of pints together in Dublin.

Blazing Paddles

The next morning was still and beautiful, they filled their stomachs with breakfast and mugs of tea and headed to the car park. In Mike's van with the kayak strapped to the roof, he felt scared and was in a surreal, fearful world, trapped inside his own body. Every bump on the road was a shock, like the van had no suspension. Detached from his senses, absent-mindedly hearing Mike saying, "We're crossing today" to the coastguard, on his phone. Something about checking in every two hours. He was in a dream, as though he'd forgotten his lines or had stepped from one reality into another for a while. The world became foreign and new in a frightening way. He absent-mindedly looked over at Mike as he drove, as if he didn't recognise him. Mike said something. He saw lips move, caught half of what was said, smiled, half laughed a 'Yeah' and looked out the window again, hoping Mike wouldn't keep talking or wasn't expecting an answer.

Porth Dafarch beach was calm and inviting – a perfect scene. There he met some of the brilliant people who had helped him make the kayaking possible through generous donations of time and money, Eddy had covered all the costs and Helen would take his bag across the sea on the ferry. He met a man with a drone who, when they launched, filmed the whole event for him and put it on YouTube (Walk for Aoife – Kayaking from Holyhead to Dun Laoghaire), to help with fundraising. When they slid away into the still morning sea, all doubts and fears drifted off, leaving him with the distilled focus he needed to tackle the task.

They stopped off at a beach soon after launch to adjust some things and excrete the last of the tea, and there they met a man walking his dog. The Irish Sea crossing story immediately activated this man's storytelling faculties. He told them there had been a lifeboat station on the cliff above and that a man from Manchester had bought it. He was a raging alcoholic, with a penchant for abusing women and collecting American cars. One day, after three bottles of whiskey he drove his car off the cliff and into the sea. The man then became a bit nostalgic and told them that he used to be a fisherman. He had the biggest boat on Holy Island. A model of a trawler he had built was in the Maritime museum in Cardiff. There was definitely a longing in his talking, as if he had missed out on something, as though that boat was the only thing that brought meaning to him at that stage in his life. He couldn't help but feel a bit sad for him, but he had really opened his heart to them in acknowledgement of their journey. It was interesting to observe what effect the journey was sometimes having on people.

There is a simple beauty to kayaking, difficult to describe. It is a low carbon way to travel, like a bicycle in a way. There is something unique about sitting at sea level and working the whole body to get somewhere. In the kayak, one uses one's legs to maintain stability, anchoring the body within the vessel, so the upper part can move as required. It is a dance between the demands of the sea and the stretch of the body. It is a symbiosis of human body and floating contraption – a thing of beauty indeed. When in the kayak it was wise to move with the boat and the sea as, like with the tractor drawing silage over potholed roads, there was that risk of something going wrong – and in a kayak, that would generally mean ending up upside down in the water.

The double kayak was necessary in their case as he had only been in a kayak twice before that day – both times having been within five weeks of the beginning of the walk. This could have been seen as a considerable risk, yet he was driven to take on the challenge in a way he had never felt drive before – there was no thought of failure. Fear, yes, but not failure. He wondered how much the memory of Aoife had to do with this feeling he had not experienced before. The sea had also called him in a way it had not before. The deep fear he had always held of drowning, of being out of his depth, was an aversion to his own depths, a fear of the unknown. He felt as if he would drown in life, like living his truth was too deep an experience for him, too risky and unknown. He had remained on the shore where he felt solid ground, but always looked longingly out towards the sea. Deep water meant participation for him, but he was not up for it until that moment.

Moving through the mellow sea with plopping paddles they crept their way towards Dublin – slower than walking pace. There was time now to take it all in, as once they had cleared the Welsh coast all that lay in front of them was 'empty' water. Five minutes out of every hour they stopped; ate, drank, peed and then continued.

Spadework

Part of what gave him the confidence to know he could find the stamina to cross the sea was the fact that he had done a lot of manual work. In his twenties, after dropping out of university and leaving a pub job he went to work outdoors, with a groundwork company whose gaffer was a regular at the pub. There he experienced a different way of work following in the tradition of Irish manual labourers in England, doing drainage and paving. The Irish had built the canals in Manchester and had been doing manual labour there for generations. Great gangs of them, he was told, lived in sheds on site and cooked great wads of bacon on sheets of steel over a fire every morning. It was a hardy and menial existence.

His experience was somewhat different. Travelling in a transit van to reach the site by 8am, laying concrete slabs on sharp sand to an engineers drawing, working with alcoholics and stooped, arthritic fifty year old Irish men from the west of Ireland. One in particular, a kind machine driver called Joe, would tell him "Get out of this game, boy!" with a warning shake of his head at every opportunity. There was a grimness to it, the history being one of necessity, it was regular work for capable Irish men, better paid than back home. He didn't mind the work, if anything there was too much waiting around for him. Waiting for things to be delivered, for the gaffer's OK on a piece of work. It was hard work, but often very dull. He was struck by the depressed state he found within everyone he worked with. The Irish fellas were mainly quiet and grumbly, they seemed lonely and stand offish. This was not healthy for him although he longed to work outdoors. He imagined what it must have been like for generations of Irish people who had worked in England for perhaps decent money, but little else. The conclusions he drew were that there was hardly one happy person within the gang he was part of, including himself. Eamonn was a cheery little man though, Manchester born but of Irish stock, his cheeks and nose had the rugged, red appearance of a seasoned drinker. There was a lightness to him and also something hidden away, which he could identify with. Eamonn often had little entertaining, child-like rhymes, one of which went "Hi diddly dee – I'd like a cup of tea. Hee diddly doo, I think you'd like one too." This was Eamonn's way of saying "Get the kettle on."

He remained with the groundwork company for a couple of months before it was time to move on, having regained his physical strength after what were ultimately dissatisfying stints at university and pub work. He looked through the Yellow Pages for landscaping firms, as he felt this might be more suitable work than doing drainage and flagging. He saw the name "Outer Space", which he liked and called that number. He started work the following week and there he learned the joy of urban outdoor work without the depressive side, with interesting conversation and trust from Iain who taught him many skills and became a good friend. The simplicity of manual work and good company in a garden was a unique feeling.

The spade, he had decided since coming to England, was a delight to handle. In Ireland, growing up, they used shovels – the ones with heart-shaped blade, akin to 'spades' of the deck of cards fame. He grew up using shovels with long, unwieldy handles – and the utilisation of the knee in the digging process always felt somewhat awkward to him. He'd got used to the English spade. It was square-bladed, almost squat in appearance compared to the Irish model with a handle at the end of a shorter wooden shaft, whose purpose was to provide purchase and perhaps to drive the blade home with whatever force was required. Somewhat more mercenary than the Irish version, but somehow this made more sense to him. It was almost as if the Irish shovel was unfinished.

Over the years he had become excavator, chipper, chopper, marker, leverer, rooter outer, leveller, hammerer and slicer with the spade, which could be adapted to any job, from digging drains to delicately removing a thin layer of turf from a lawn. He took pride in his spadework and used the tool so often in his landscaping work it felt like his weapon of choice, as a warrior would use a sword. It was a tool of exploration and wonder - unearthing, revealing, allowing access to what the hands couldn't reach, helping him to explore his own strength and skill. Using a spade well was about timing and accuracy, there was rhythm involved and a purpose to digging out a space to lay a patio or lawn. It was an art to be mastered. Digging and stripping the soil to find the finish level, akin to exploring his mind and reality through play, as a child does. Breathing in outdoor air, getting a sweat on, feeling his body working the land. The spade was the tool he loved to do this with. He dug a lot in his twenties, when he had felt most lost, when he thought everything he did was wrong, but didn't know how to deal with thoughts of loss and anxiety for a world he felt disconnected from. Digging was something he always got right – it made sense. He needed that work rather than the money – he was saved by the spade, he dug and divined.

Lazy S

The 'lazy S' was the shape their journey took – so named because of the tides. As they travelled due west they would become involved in the tidal flow, north into the Atlantic for six hours and then south again, meaning that every six hours on their journey they would drift up to a mile either side of their due west 'line' from Porth Dafarch to Dun Laoghaire – that line also being a busy shipping lane.

Three hours into the paddle and a northerly wind picked up. He felt the struggle coming on and an uneasy feeling started to rise within him. It was choppy and bumpy, they needed to focus and push through. He began to feel frustrated, wondering why it had to be so difficult. He felt irritable. His vest felt tight as did his stomach, and he began to feel doubt creeping in. There was no talking for the next three hours as he and Mike focused. The boat thumped through the waves and at times his paddle was not connecting with water. It felt unpredictable and difficult. Even after adjusting his life vest it still felt tight and uncomfortable. The wind then dropped almost as suddenly as it had begun and everything felt ok again. The knot in his stomach disappeared, his mood lifted and he began to feel that it was likely he had been seasick – the contrast between how he had felt with the wind and without. How his thoughts automatically went into negativity and doubt and just as quickly left them behind again was curious to him – it was as if he had no control of his thinking, like the thoughts were whirring away in there, ready to take him down at the first sight of a bit of choppy water and the feeling of uncertainty.

More hours went by; paddling, stopping for five minutes to eat, pee and bail out – the little boat was taking on a small amount of water as they travelled, so emptying that out became part of their routine. At that stage the very gently rolling, rippling water was all that could be seen in every direction – Wales was far behind and Dublin yet to appear. The water reflected the sky above and together, sea and sky made a calming, soporific blue-green surround that was altogether soothing and supportive. Even breathing felt different, as if the sea and sky were filling him up with each breath and the gentle, watery undulations were deeply calming and supportive. It was dreamlike, and he felt the emptiness of sound as it disappeared towards the horizon, with nothing to reflect it.

The Search for Still Waters

Mike's strangely muffled country music was playing through a speaker in a tupperware container to keep it dry, adding a surreal, 1980's picnic feel to the scene. Although not his first choice, the music was well suited to the moment – with songs of love and loss projected out into the emptiness of the blue scene was made more surreal by seeing the occasional silent ship on the horizon, looking like tiny toys. They truly were in open waters, perhaps twenty miles from land – in that tiny vessel.

He witnessed the sun's creep west, unhindered by cloud and felt what it was like to travel in one set direction for hours, without distraction. It seemed the sun was overtaking them as they went across the empty sea. There was the feeling of the earth moving – if the sun moved forward, were they going backward? Feeling the forward movement, he wondered about the point of travel, the influence of tides and of getting somewhere and then the bigger picture of movement, outside of his journey. At that moment were they paddling uphill or across, as gravity held them on the water, were they upside down, as the planet sped through space? What was travel, really? There was the idea of going somewhere, but where was the sea going? Where was the world going? What were they doing in a floating container, within a larger container, floating in space and what is *that* contained within?

A great surging sound suddenly came at them from behind, like a boat ploughing the waves and he felt panic rise as their tiny boat was violently rocked. Rapid thoughts of panic ensued before any action could be taken. Could it be a ship that hadn't seen them? What the hell was going on?! And then, almost as quickly, all went calm again. They looked around for any trace of a ship, which might have come upon them from nowhere, their tiny vessel barely visible on the sea. But there was no boat and in the seconds that followed they looked to the sea and to each other for an explanation for the freak wave – and then it came. As the grey mass slowly broke through the water's surface, his face changed from puzzlement to joy as the minke whale emerged and spumed what could only be described as a greeting to them through its blowhole. The wholeness of that sound in the still, country music-filled air struck him with its beauty and he knew it was for them. The whale had come to see them, the only boat for miles around, propelled by a pair of paddles held by a crew of two. It disappeared back beneath just as quickly as it had come, wonder and awe replacing the panic. He felt taken care of again, in some way. His sister came to mind, a solo traveller on a journey, acknowledging them for their effort and commitment, a whopping great omen for safe passage.

He occasionally saw seabirds as they travelled, one species in particular he guessed was the manx shearwater – a graceful bird whose purpose and power came through rapid, stiff wingbeats, travelling at great speed, practically skimming across the surface of the open sea. They were a joy to watch with their long, narrow, aerodynamic wings, made for strong wind and wet conditions. He had never seen such grace in a bird despite watching gannets and shags or ducky divers, as his father called them, dive for fish in Dingle bay, as a child. This was something he hadn't witnessed before –

the behavior of the birds on the open water highway – the beauty of their shape and movement, often the only sight on the otherwise calming sea. They travelled with speed and poise, wings like blades, thoroughly at home on the water.

Hours passed and Ireland slowly emerged from the horizon. The journey was epic, but the land ahead kept them focused as daylight receded. Dublin's lights twinkled tantalisingly near, but all the same they knew they were still a long way off and had a whole night of work ahead. He could see hills in the distance and felt the pull of Ireland. They would see occasional ships, looking impossibly large, travelling the same line as them, sometimes to their north, at times much closer and then, to the south as the tidal flow created their 'lazy S' shape across the sea.

Twelve hours in and they neared darkness. They slowly chased the sun's last rays west and were then alone on a murky sea as Ireland's lights became their beacon. Then, as if out of nowhere, more ships started to creep in. They appeared to come from all directions, as huge clusters of lights, like giant nocturnal creatures grazing the dark sea. The two men had to stop in their tiny craft to gauge the direction the ships were coming from, occasionally having to take evasive action, deciding their tiny boat and head torches might not be noticed by a huge ship, hundreds of feet long – a floating town, a hulking mass of steel. One came a little too close and they sat there watching as its bulk floated past, the sound of the water being churned up by its giant propellers, their tiny craft bobbing in its wake.

The Unknown Universe

At around midnight, long after Mike's iPod had run out of juice, they were tiring after fourteen hours at sea. Finding themselves in the middle of shipping lanes in the dark felt intense, but soon they seemed to be through the difficult part. They pushed on, Ireland feeling closer each hour and at around two in the morning Mike took out the map to check how far from shore they were. They were optimistic but it was difficult to judge by the shore lights. It turned out they were still eighteen miles from Dublin. Realizing that they were only just over two thirds of the way and already exhausted, his heart sank deep into the depths below. What had felt like an already arduous journey was beginning to feel like a torturous ordeal. What was more, the tidal flow had taken them far north of Dublin and so they had to push south-west to find the bay mouth, still many miles south. At this point the sea became choppy again and progress felt slow, riding the waves, despite a following wind. He wanted to leave the stupid kayak, couldn't believe he had got himself into such a crazy situation – his body was in pain and his mind was screaming at him to get out and run. He wanted to leave the boat and run ashore. The impulse was strong. He was stuck there, sitting, after hours and hours of sitting and there was nothing else to do but sit and paddle.

Then, in a moment of desperation he started to sing. He felt self-conscious, having only sung alone before when struggling. He knew there was something in it, as he remembered from walking across Anglesey a couple of days before, in another reality. Beyond hopelessness, fatigue and pain was song. They both sang. He sang the sea shanties he loved from when he was a child and he felt the strength return. Actual physical strength was summoned through singing! It was mysterious and beautiful. Both sang for at least an hour, Mike sang country ballads – songs with an impossible depth of sadness and loss that felt supremely meaningful in those moments. They sang whatever came into their heads and it pushed them forward through the waves, reconnected them with their resolve and, through that dark night on the Irish Sea, two eerie voices could be heard, singing into waves, into their bodies, for strength.

When it began to get light they were at Dublin Bay, its huge mouth, over ten miles wide was open to them. They pointed their boat towards where Dun Laoghaire lay, yet to be seen. As dawn crept in, the grey sea was dark and uninviting, concrete looking waves were holding them back, illusions of land were appearing and disappearing. His vision was creating land to help him feel he was near and a sense of desperation to end the journey was strong. They pushed forward, trying to reach solid ground. Feeling too tired to continue, his hands set into claws around the paddle shaft hours before. He was barely holding the paddle at this stage – his grip had almost failed him, but for the fact that his hands had cramped into hook shapes, the paddle would have floated off. He could hear the clunk as his paddle repeatedly hit the side of the boat – his stroke shortening. He heard Mike pushing him from behind, encouraging him to dig deep again. This was the final bit, the last few miles and it was as hard as he could imagine.

Land appeared and disappeared in front of them, and he had to shake his head to free it from the hallucinations. It was difficult to focus or judge distance – Dublin looked so close yet they were so tiny and slow it felt like they would never get there. Time wasn't making sense. Minutes felt like hours, hours felt like days. They pushed on, feeling like the land was getting no closer, as if they were firmly anchored at bay and a sick joke was being played on them and they were just paddling on the spot. They agreed to push ahead and put everything they had into it for a further hour, again feeling exhausted and no closer.

Then it happened. The concrete mass of Dun Laoghaire's east pier actually appeared ahead of them, as if it had been hiding. At the same moment the water seemed to calm and they felt like they were moving again. Had it really been so choppy and difficult or was it desperation that made him feel that way? The feelings of panic and agony subsided, their pace steadied, relief washed over him. They savoured the last calming moments, drifting towards the pier on a relaxing, Monday morning paddle. The journey was behind them.

They saw a point on the pier that looked like a ramp and aimed for it. When they got there it was steep and would be a hard landing, but they were determined to make land. As the little plastic boat clunked against the side he heaved himself out and collapsed on the concrete, Mike followed and they hauled the heavy kayak up the steep ramp and on to the pier wall. They had done it! The first thing they saw was the still water of the harbour, realising that their desperation to hit land had brought them to the outside of the pier and they would have to carry what felt like an impossibly heavy kayak for around five hundred metres, to the shore end. They had done it though! 8.30 in the morning and they were twenty two hours and sixty miles from Porth Dafarch in Wales. It was warm and sunny, and they were both soaked to the skin and exhausted.

That moment changed him. He had achieved something big, had broken through pain and giving up, and through not having a choice had found a powerful resolve, like he'd never felt before. He had dug deep. He'd been so afraid of failure all his life, it was as if there had been no other option for him. Failure was a label, not a fixed truth, and from that experience he began to see his life a little bit differently, just like when he first saw that his world was made of thoughts, which did not define who he was. Crossing sixty miles of open water - and having drunk only one litre of water that whole time because having a pee was such a protracted process - he was more inspired (and dehydrated) than he had ever been in his life. And hungry. Hungry and inspired and dehydrated. Different. Stirred up, in some way.

You Have to Laugh

His contact in Dublin was Dee, a good friend of his sister's. He gave Dee a call to say they had landed. She was very matter of fact and far too alert for his state of being in that moment. All he can remember from the haze of that conversation was her saying "Didn't you know that the ferry stopped going from Dun Laoghaire about 18 months ago?" There was a pause. He had no words. Or thoughts. His brain began overheating on learning this one small, yet crucial detail, which he had overlooked. "Are you sure you're related to your sister?" said Dee with an inquisitive tone. That didn't feel so helpful to him in that moment, but he managed a laugh all the same. "We all have our own individual strengths" he replied and they said goodbye for the moment.

As they struggled along the pier with the weirdly heavy kayak they saw a jeep coming towards them. "Here we go", he mumbled to Mike, as the Harbour Police vehicle pulled up right next to them. He considered how strange the scene might look; two exhausted looking men wrestling a kayak along the east pier. He wondered what the implications were for going from one country to another without having passports checked or following any official border crossing rules. It looked like they were about to find out. As if it wasn't complicated enough, what with landing on the choppy side of the pier, having no idea how to get to the ferry and having to carry a kayak neither had the strength to carry, for nearly half a mile.

Two men got out, one in uniform, the other plain clothed. The plain clothed man approached them, smiling, with his hand outstretched and said "Welcome!" It was Dee's dad, Paddy. Phew! He had dragged the harbour police in to help and had filled them in on the journey as he commandeered the police vehicle. The officer shook his hand and offered a cup of tea. He and Mike looked at each other, acknowledging this surreal, amusing moment on that pier and were relieved to see the first friendly faces presented to them in Ireland. The harbour policeman was far more enthusiastic about their trip than they could manage to be in that moment.

Paddy jumped into action telling them there was a van on the way. The van turned up minutes later and the driver was keen and ready. He and Mike looked at each other again and then at the small van thinking the same thing. How is an eighteen-foot kayak going to fit in the ten-foot loading bay? It was simple. They put the kayak into the van, tied it all together and the kayak stuck almost halfway out, looking like it could slide out at any second. It wouldn't of course as the driver had securely tied all his ropes and within minutes what seemed like too big a mission for them was shared and being taken care of. They agreed on the spot that the driver would take Mike the seven miles to the ferry straight away, shattering their romantic idea of some rest and a couple of pints together. So they hugged goodbye, Mike was whisked off to the ferry terminal and he was taken away to Paddy's house for some sleep.

He felt like a complete zombie. Paddy was talking to him in the car on the way back to the house, but he could barely focus on what Paddy was saying. Not only had he not had any sleep for 28 hours, he had had the biggest adventure of his life in that time. Back at the house he was pleased to see his rucksack sitting there, thanks to Helen. He thought about Mike, who he barely knew yet who trusted him to have what it took to cross the sea together. Mike was a rare kind of guy.

As he got ready to go to sleep, social media reminded him that it was exactly one year to the day since he had learned to swim out of his depth.

Keep Going

The next day was spent in a haze of tiredness and hunger – he had a walk back down to Dun Laoghaire harbour and felt a sense of great achievement. He later shared a massive meal (two or three helpings) and hearty conversation round at Dee's – including his first recounting of the crossing story. To be welcomed and looked after by people he didn't know, but who felt like family, was a bonus.

The following day as he walked through Dublin and out the other side, observing the difference in manhole covers. Banners and reminders from the 100th anniversary of the Easter Rising remained on buildings. It struck him as poignant that, although he felt little connection with his capital city, he was reminded of the freedom for which his ancestors had fought, and that he could now walk (and kayak) freely from Britain to Ireland, without persecution or judgement, because of the people who came before. This freedom had been given without expectation. He recalled his mother's family who worked the land, and the many priests, nuns and brothers the family produced – people doing God's work for the preservation of morale, to educate, care for and guide people. It was humbling to walk past these reminders. He became aware of his guilt for what felt like running away twenty years before. Although he had been home many times, Irish culture had changed dramatically and almost beyond recognition for him and in the next two weeks of walking, he would be rediscovering that.

He was glad to leave the city. The Grand Canal would take him west for the next few days. He stayed in Clondalkin with kind relatives that night, sleeping better than he had the whole journey and left feeling rested. His blisters had benefitted from the two-day break and were no longer painful. He had pushed through. The kayak journey already felt hazy and distant, now he was back on the trail again. He passed under small bridges, which led to towns and villages he had never heard of; Hazelhatch, Ardclough, Alexandra Bridge. The grand looking Lyons Estate, its high walls and many entrances along the canal gave an air of mystery and importance. He was beginning to realise how little he knew of the country he grew up in and of the people that inhabited it. He was only 19 years old when he had left.

There was a cafe right on the canal at the Lyons Estate, which looked perfectly tranquil and was due to open at midday. It was 11.40. He stood there for a minute, imagining himself sitting outside with a coffee and an immaculately prepared sandwich. He stared at the door, willing it to open 20 minutes early because he knew he wouldn't stop there. Splitting up his walking time with cafe outings didn't feel right. This was his job and he needed to get back to work.

He came off the canal around Ardclough in the hope of finding a shop. Less than 5 minutes up the road a small, local convenience store was where he found lunch. From outside it looked more like a country cottage with a car park in place of a front garden. He chatted to the man behind the counter, telling him about his journey. He paid for his food and the man gave him €10 towards the fundraising.

He messaged Beth. She and Rae were putting make-up on each other. He was glad to be able to experience his family when on the road. To have them with him in an instant kept him going. Through Beth's support the journey became possible for him. He sometimes didn't notice what an effect she had on his whole journey. When he decided to do it, she was on board and it didn't take any convincing. She never mentioned once about how much it would take for her to have their daughter on her own for a whole month while her husband was gallivanting around the place. She believed in him completely and that love and support was the best thing he could have imagined - so much so that he almost took it for granted. Beth would send him photos of her and Rae with crazy clown make-up on and little sound files of Rae saying 'Goodnight, Daddy'. They attempted internet phone calls, but often the signal was so poor that they would never get to talk for more than a minute before the beeps came in. They had many a frustrating conversation like that, but it was still good to have the messages and photos, and occasionally the odd video clip. He was never that far away from his clan, and they kept him company when he needed them.

On that day they messaged back and forth about leaving Manchester and moving to Anglesey, with its varied and rich habitat and its fantastic geology and history. They were fantasising about buying some land and having a place of their own, between photos of tiger make-up and Rae cuddling the dog. It was exciting to dream about change and they were both keen to do something. On the road it was hard to imagine being back in Manchester, the place he had 'walked away' from.

He then listened to a book for a while to calm his mind. As his busy head got a bit quieter he also became aware that the towpath had narrowed to a thin track and he wouldn't hear people coming up from behind. He popped the headphones out and almost immediately a guy on a bike came up behind him. He stopped and they chatted for a bit. He was heading from Dublin to Galway, following the canal for 80 miles, then the mighty river Shannon after that. He said that the landscape became more dramatic after the canal, as he'd travelled it before. He was the kind of guy who appeared to have nothing to lose and he told him about his journey, which the man liked the sound of. There was no confusion or sense of 'why are you doing this?' about this man, like he'd had from many other people. He got it and loved it, no explanation needed and it was a pleasure talking to him in that moment. He looked at the battered old mountain bike and scruffy clothes, his apparent lack of gear and thought 'This guy's a bit mad.' Then he laughed when he realised how mad *he* was. They had a nice, short chat - two souls on a journey, excited about what was happening - and then the guy rode away.

Learning about Grief and Connection

He got to lock number 14, where he was due to meet his cousin Anne, occasionally wondering if the guy on the bike actually existed or whether that encounter had happened on a different plane, like meeting a later version of himself, or a spirit guide or a ghost. He gave Anne a call. She came and met him by the bridge. They immediately hit it off and, walking down the road the conversation quickly veered towards mindfulness.

The bridge was limestone, different shades of grey with flecks of white, a tight hump on a bend. He thought about who must have built that bridge in a time before tight bends mattered, the type of bridge built long before cars were invented, some with deadly, blind bends built in. Others had tight, almost comical humps, as if those bridges had contracted over the generations. Anne pointed out the grooves where the sliding ropes of horse drawn barges had rubbed U-shaped, channelled grooves into the square cut stone on the side of the bridge. He imagined the one-inch thick ropes, creaking and zipping as they dragged their way through, cutting into the mottled grey masonry over the decades. He thought of the people of that time, with canal barges and horses trotting about on stony roads, the canal towpath being the main thoroughfare. He wondered what their lives were like, if they had worn rough woollen clothing, and boots that chafed and blistered.

As they got up on to the road they had to practically throw themselves against the ditch as cars flew past. After a full day on the solitary canal he had forgotten about traffic, with nothing but still water, plants and birds to keep him company. Anne was pointing out neighbours as they travelled slowly along. "I like to keep the gate closed" she said as they got to hers. A solid, friendly looking bungalow sat almost hidden amongst trees and wildlife. There was an air of the jungle about it - a dampness and seclusion. He liked the feeling he got from the place; like a robin's nest, hidden away in the undergrowth. Anne had an air of magic about her and he was instantly excited to be spending time there. She showed him to his room. He dropped his bag and they started chatting. She asked him if he was interested in hearing about family, as he made himself a sandwich.

Anne took him on a journey through blurred black and white prints in many photo albums and named every person, most of whom he had never heard of. He relished the whole experience, although knowing he wouldn't remember any of the details – it was all in the telling.

He also took the opportunity to share about his sisters, who Anne had heard about but didn't know, including Aoife. He was able to share his feelings about Aoife and what he had carried with him all his life, which had kept him in a certain headspace and which therapies he had tried in order to sort it out. Anne then talked about her own husband and how he had died young, leaving her with two small children, who were five and seven at the time. Anne was upbeat considering what she'd been through. She was completely open and he got something deep from her sharing, like she was communing with the spirits. It was as though she was in touch with something 'other' from all she had suffered.

It was a little cool in the house and Anne set the fire and lit it. She was keen for him to be cosy and he sat down by the warming fire to write a bit. It was unexpected to have the fire on a sunny May day, but it felt like just what he needed. He observed the tiled fireplace with its cast iron grate and fireside toolset all hooked on their stand. It felt rustic and personal, it was a privilege to be sitting in that space.

Lost and Found

His parents phoned and they talked for half an hour about logistics, which direction he was going in and where he'd end up next. It was all feeling a bit much for him and he realised he had to lean on his dad quite a bit for support, which he didn't want him to feel the strain of. The dream of camping and being self-sufficient all the way was well and truly out the window and now he was submitting to being helped all the way home. He realised, when talking to his father that he hadn't even looked at the map of Ireland properly at that stage and was even confused about the direction he was going the following day. He hadn't put any time into planning the Irish part of the journey and wanted to crawl into a hole in that moment. The Grand Canal branched off, one arm heading south west (the natural direction of home) and the other, due west. It made sense for him to head south west although when he actually looked at his options - places to stay and people he knew began to run out shortly after that. He decided to take the west-going branch to Tullamore and go south from there. There were options for trails in Ireland, but that sort of journey would mean going off the beaten track quite a bit, and would lessen his options for accommodation. West was definitely the best.

He felt a bit silly in that moment, as if he didn't really know what was going on and his parents were telling him what to do, so he naturally felt like he should be rebelling against it. Of course, what they were telling him was the only sensible option so he went along with it. What he later would recognise as fatigue and physical depletion was at that time just a feeling of helplessness, confusion and embarrassment. It was still unknown where he would be staying or sleeping in the following days, although this would turn out to bring him many surprises. At the time though, he worried that people thought he was a bit useless. It was time to be open to spontaneity, to be more whimsical and allow uncertainty to be part of the plan – or the entire plan, even.

He went to bed feeling good after the evening's chatting and laughter with Anne and Maria, her daughter. They ate chocolate cake and drank wine. Maria had already left to tend to her horses by the time he got up the next morning. He and Anne had breakfast and he made himself a sandwich for the road. She walked him back down to the canal and showed him the place as she saw it - an ever-changing world of potential, possibility and natural beauty. He felt her relationship with that place.

She took him through the ruins of an old house, built over a stream, a deep pool before it flowed over a weir. They flitted from one scene to another, each illuminated by her imagination. He took a photo and then went on his way with a spring in his step. He felt light again and ready. Anne wished him well and hoped that he would not run into too much wet ground as she had heard that the canal was less well maintained further on. He thanked her and was interested in the mystery the canal held for her and how he could explore it for her in the following days.

Anne's sharing of her grief story was like a dip in a cool pond for him – hearing her talk openly about death and loss was both refreshing and struck him deeply, probably because he had always avoided grief talk. Firstly, he didn't feel important enough to be part of that conversation because he didn't recognise that it had happened to him. He felt that somehow his story was different, unworthy, his grief not worth sharing. Perhaps it was more that his story was surrounded with shame, because of his relationship with Aoife, and the shame clouded his feelings about it. Anne's story was a privilege to hear and he knew why he was now 'lost' in that place, uncertain of a way forward. He went there to learn about grief and begin to move through that.

The canal was beautiful all along the stretch after Sallins, the country flat, green and lush in its springtime garb. Further along, the canal became more the heart of the area, towpaths turning into roads with houses built along both sides of the water. He met three serious looking walkers and they walked together for a time. They were heading to the Spanish part of the

The Search for Still Waters

Camino Di Santiago in July – a pilgrimage walking route he had first heard about in the pub, thinking that sort of thing was for someone else. He got caught up in the excitement of their walk. They were great company for a while and it was another opportunity to share about his own pilgrimage and the story of his sister. Sharing the journey with strangers made it feel more purposeful. It gave him strength to see such people, laugh and chat, and he felt once again like he was doing something bigger than himself - not just walking along in his own little world. At the same time he thought about the Camino Di Santiago and how people go there purposefully to connect with the journey – each carrying their own baggage, so to speak, and how those journeys can be a shared experience for the participants. There he was, on his own journey, laughing to himself about the madness of it all – how weird it was, in the quieter moments to think he was actually doing it, that he had gone so far – that he was walking 'home'.

He spent some time thinking about how it was to live apart from Aoife, as a child, and who she was to him. He had begun to think about her with fond memories rather than tragic. His perspective was beginning to change a bit. He felt brighter, and having talked to James, Bryn, Anne and Maria and even 'the Camino ladies' gave him insight. He saw that there's never a need to hold on to pain, and one of the main reasons he felt so separate from those around him was because he didn't trust that they could be part of his healing process. His perspective was changing and he was beginning to see what holding on to pain and grief was doing to him. It was shutting him down to the possibility of connection and a richer life. He promised himself that he would cease that habit and start to let go. As a kid he had chosen sadness, he decided to be unhappy about his situation for his own reasons, and that gave him a filter through which he saw everything. There was a way for him to find the sadness in every situation. Was all this sadness because he misunderstood how he could have loved his sister more? Instead, he chose to grieve for her all her life. He was beginning to get a clearer picture of his feelings.

Griefland

There were many gravestones or memorial stones by the side of the canal. Memories of people who had died there, it appeared. They had a tragic air about them for him. Were they drowned? That stretch of canal brought a deep melancholy; houses stood shyly behind hedges and high walls, guarded by invisible barking dogs. He liked the somewhat eerie, canalside culture, with its gravestones - a daily reminder for everyone who passed by. Also, his mental state had shifted, not having been anywhere near a town for around 40 miles of walking, and having talked about death and dying in a new way, the previous day. He felt he was seeing a different, hidden part of Ireland in that moment; a ghostly, isolated land of loss. This may have just been a giant 'grief-mirror' for him, passing through 'death world.'

That day had felt like a long one and his aim of reaching Edenderry no longer felt feasible. There was something about being alone on the canal with his thoughts that made it feel longer, but necessarily so. As if the track was taking its time teaching him. Some days the lesson was easy - others were long and arduous. Sometimes when he had company the day went quickly and sometimes more slowly. There was no formula or set way of experiencing it, and often the number of hours did not reflect the number of miles walked. He had walked 12 miles in 9 hours with stinging blisters and discomfort and he had walked 15 miles in almost half that time. But his conditions were changing the whole time. One thing he was learning was that pain and discomfort were only states of mind and he felt like he could walk his way through anything if he wanted. He no longer felt any doubt about reaching home and could even see himself completing the journey in a wheelchair (slightly cheating, perhaps) or crutches if he had to. The resolve was strong.

He was looking forward to seeing Rita, the first person from Dingle he would meet on the walk. She was a teacher in Offaly and lived there with Arthur and their family. They'd had some email contact along the way regarding logistics, etc. He had, in his disorganised state, been unable to give her exact dates until the day before his arrival date. She got in touch with him by email a couple of days before he did the crossing, which began, "Hi, wherever you might be at present. I'm fascinated by your latest escapade..."

He called Rita from near one of the humpy bridges, just as it began to rain. She said she knew where he was and would meet him by that bridge. She would be around 45 minutes. He perched on a low, crumbling wall and ate chocolate, fruit and nuts, and quietly debated walking for another 45 minutes. It would take him a few more miles closer to his aim of Edenderry, which he had fallen well short of. Sitting on the wall, he savoured the light rain plopping, dripping down through the large horse chestnut leaves, appreciative of their shelter in that moment of peace next to the bridge. There were a few houses around and the occasional car climbed the blind hump, he had momentary anxiety as he felt a car would hit him, then relief as each car would correct its course when visibility returned.

Then he noticed the swallows as they swooped, fluttered and played round the bridge. The cars came and went over the steep arch, the birds splendidly weaved their way around them, wheeling and reeling, dodging and skimming. It was such a show despite the rain, or perhaps because of it. He felt privileged to be there, witnessing that scene. The birds were definitely enjoying themselves and their playing set something off in him. It made him wish to play more and he reflected on how much he may be missing out on by being depressed and taking himself so seriously. Sitting there on that low stone wall, resting his bones and feet, knowing he had done enough walking for one day, he acknowledged the work it took for him to get to that moment. What was supposed to be waiting for a lift had become witnessing a beautiful scene, a perfect composition of avian aerobatics in a quiet, country place, with school kids being dropped off next to the canal, water and old buildings around him. A sense of peace enveloped him.

The Search for Still Waters

An old lady walking a shihtzu proceeded along slowly. She was wearing makeup and a raincoat, red lipstick on lips no longer visible. She opened with a warning: "Be careful on that wall". A lorry had crashed into it the previous day, knocking some of it over. She said she was going on holiday soon with her family for a few days. He couldn't help wonder what kind of life she'd had - the hardship felt apparent to him, in her drawn face and stooping gait. He wondered how often she left that quiet, peaceful place by the canal and how the outside world felt to her.

He mentioned the swallows to her and his words floated away as if he had not spoken them. There was no response. Perhaps she didn't notice them or perhaps couldn't see them or maybe they were her swallows, she had brought them there to play. Her short walk with the dog told him that she wasn't used to going far. There appeared to be a toughness to her, a side which reminded him of his grandmother, that long-suffering, Catholic persona of hard work and little opportunity.

His grandmother, born in 1905, while Ireland was still under British rule, would have remembered the 1916 Rising, the civil war and the Free State. She experienced poverty and struggle most of her life, she moved from a village only 4 miles away to an arranged marriage with his grandfather. He realised he knew nothing of her life and whether she had good or poor fortune, but by the sound of it, her life was one of work and commitment and little social life other than that of her immediate family. He realised again how fortunate he was to be making his journey – to indulge his emotions, intellect and body, heal his hurts and bring light to his confusions. He was also doing this journey for all of them – his ancestors who toiled and struggled, lived with oppression and worked to within an inch of their lives to survive. They came through all of that so he could be there, facing his grief and the pain they themselves could perhaps not face. And he felt that pain, as a child. The residue of hardship and toil, the resentment of oppression, the vast difference within two generations of a rural Irish peasant lineage and the new world of opportunity which flooded in around them as he was growing up. The idea that they didn't have to hold on anymore, that the old ways were dying, making way for new things. Not better or worse, just new. He felt grateful that his ancestors had come through their struggles so he could make that journey. Or perhaps he had imagined that old woman, like the guy on the bike.

Embrace the Pain

A white car rounded the corner, and he heard the pipping of its horn. It could only be Rita. She pulled in and hopped out of the car with a big smile. "Throw your stuff in the back, there" she said, cheerfully, in a brogue that could only be described as "*Wesht* Kerry". He got in and sat down and got the feeling of excitement and energy, which Rita brought to any occasion. She wanted to explore the area a bit as she wasn't exactly sure what the place was about, so they headed off down the road for a nosey around the neighbourhood. "Ah sure, how *are* ya?" she said, in her uniquely charming way. She was exactly the same as always, which was delightful.

They explored the area like a couple of kids out for a joyride in their parents' car after school.

They chatted excitedly whilst driving back to the house in Clonbullogue. The landscape was green but with patches of dark brown, the peat bogs coming up every now and again. He could tell Rita was proud to be living there and she talked about the locals with affection and as a local herself.

The rain had stopped and the evening was starting to look fine and settled. He felt worn out, like the day was too much. It was only a bit of walking, he reassured himself and he wasn't exactly pushing hard. The going was easy and there were few obstacles but he felt tired. He decided that he was still tired from the kayaking, which he had finished fewer than 5 days previously.

When Arthur came home they chatted a bit about vegetable growing, land and cattle, and they had bacon and cabbage for dinner. The scene felt very traditional and reminded him somewhat of what he'd grown up with. This felt both comforting and familiar - he knew he wouldn't have to be concerned about fitting in.

He sloped off to bed early, but before bed he spent a few minutes appreciating the view of mature oaks and sycamores from the bedroom window, wondering what his life would be like if he had a view like that out of his window. As he drank in the orange tinged evening light, the trees and the swifts reeling as they swooped for insects in the damp, rainwashed fields out the back. Would he ever be lucky enough to wake up to such a view each day?

The next morning he was up early. Rita cooked breakfast and he made himself lunch. She insisted that he use any food that was available and he gingerly used some fridge contents for sandwiches. He was still getting used to being somewhere different almost every day. The generosity and openness of people who let him take what he wanted from their supplies was probably not a big deal for them, but for him there wasn't much more to life at that moment than eating, walking and sleeping. After breakfast, Rita dropped him off at the bridge he was picked up from the previous day.

That morning he felt the stillness of the canalside walk. It was flat, occasionally boggy and very quiet, and save for a few trees there was nothing tall in the landscape. It was sunny and warm and almost cloudless, but then slowly, white clouds built up, followed by a wall of dark grey until the whole horizon looked ready to burst. Then it passed. It went on like this, teasing him for the whole morning, but no rain came, despite feeling very close.

He could see a long way into the distance, the brown scars of the bogs, which were used for peat harvesting, were regular. He wondered how much longer it would be until all the turf was removed and people would have to find another way of heating their homes. It was somewhat sad to see the vast turf bogs with their built in, narrow gauge railways and specialised machinery. He reflected upon resource exploitation and how when people find something of value to dig up, slaughter or exploit, that exploitation often keeps happening until there is nothing left. Humans do it with people and resources, and in many ways it is the foundation of the current state of evolution.

He was glad however to see plenty of wildlife along the canal, being charmed by the damselflies and dragonflies, and even hearing a cuckoo in the distance; the first he had heard since he was a child in Dingle. He had a vague memory of his father hushing him and pointing towards some undefined distant place from which the cuckoo call came. In that moment he felt cemented to the spot, anchored, straining to hear the next 'kwoo koo', each one brought an inner smile. He also thought about the love/hate relationship, which is easy to have with the cuckoo. About how once learning of the cuckoo's behaviour, he was helped to feel quite disgusted. How could a bird lay its egg in another's nest, then when the egg hatched the chick might roll the other eggs out and be in control of the demands of its feeder who would, inevitably, run itself ragged feeding the often disproportionately large chick? This allowed the cuckoo to both have the cross pollination of being reared by another species and be totally free of parental duties.

There was a heron high up in a birch tree and it crouched, ready to flee as he walked past. Another heron appeared on the towpath ahead. He hoped to get closer and maybe take a photo, but as he approached it would awkwardly take flight – as only a heron can. It landed another fifty metres ahead and the same situation of take off and landing kept happening. He began to feel a bit embarrassed for the poor heron. This happened five times or more until it finally acquired the nouse to head for the opposite side. He laughed at their clumsy interaction, like they were playing some kind of inane, predictable game — too simple to be anything but fun. He noted the sharp, deadly beak and long legs of the heron, made for hunting in water. It had a dinosaur-ish look about it and its screech was delightfully cretaceous in nature, he thought. That was his only interaction in those first ten miles.

He met Rita at Rode. They walked and talked about Dingle and Aoife and how it had been for him, growing up with Aoife as a sister. They spoke about her children and she told him that they had lost a child, called Mikey, when he was only fifty days old. He was born with a rare heart condition called Hypoplastic Left Heart Syndrome. With that condition, the heart only half-develops in the womb and life expectancy is often low. Rita talked with such openness and acceptance about their tiny little boy's life and death. She firmly believed that he was only meant to be with them for that time and that was it. There was no regret or bitterness and very little sadness in her voice. He realised this was perspective he needed to hear. He was held in the power of Rita's openness, along with the unexpected, beautiful, sad, uplifting story of Mikey.

It was obvious that Rita and her family had suffered great loss, but she had only positive things to say about her experience. So how did she come through it with such a beautiful perspective? "Support", she told him. Her husband Arthur held her when times were toughest and allowed her space to grieve and see the process as something beautiful. Perhaps her curious, caring nature may have gone a long way towards that, too. Rita didn't feel that Mikey was a sick baby who died, she believed he brought them something deeper, something no other person could bring and part of that was how his life brought out empathy and kindness in others. There was constant support from the community during his short life, which also led her to see the good in what was happening and accept it as so. People were praying for his life and telling her about it and she was seeing humanity at its best and the way rural Irish culture can still deal openly with death and dying. Mikey was a gift to the world and when he died his heart was donated to medical research – another fact Rita was proud of – that her boy had also made a contribution to medical science through his life and death. There was so much to be grateful for and he understood all of that, talking to Rita.

He was filled up in a way he never imagined. He felt the weight of grief he still carried about Aoife's life. He felt another shift that day as they walked along. There were similarities between Rita's situation and his parents' and he felt more empathy for his mother and father. They had to accept the news of Aoife's condition and deal with the stress of her first year with all it entailed - the pneumonia and constantly travelling to and from hospital with her whilst living in a rural place far from hospitals and medical care. Aoife's existence had felt like a heavy weight for him and here he was, literally being shown the light. It wasn't without its pain or grief, of course, but how Rita and Arthur dealt with Mikey's condition felt powerful and inspiring.

He was being given the opportunity to look with fresh eyes at what had happened almost forty years ago. He wondered how these situations were appearing for him, and his parents helping him plan his route, was leading him to these deeper experiences. He once again appreciated the space to have these experiences and felt like the point of being there in that moment was clear and powerfully connected to his journey. He had talked to both Anne and Rita about pain and loss and had learned plenty. He put himself in a position of having conversations he would normally have avoided due to his own pain.

They also talked about bogs and turf and Rita was determined, once they had got to their destination for the day, that she would somehow show him the turf cutting process. Rita explained that the semi state body Bord Na Móna owned the majority of bogs in the area. They employed a lot of people and harvested peat for power stations, horticulture and agriculture. Peat harvesting was big business in the flat, boggy midlands and, from time to time, while they walked, the dark brown of bog was the dominant landscape in every direction. Bord Na Móna had a network of narrow gauge railways set up to bring much of the milled peat to power plants to make electricity. It was also made into briquettes to heat homes. But the days of using this carbon heavy resource were coming to a close, and Ireland has since stopped harvesting peat for home consumption and electricity generation.

A Piece of Pie

That evening, Arthur's mother came round with 'Granny's apple pie' and they all had double helpings with ice cream and custard. Granny gave him 10 euro and an affectionate hug, and wished him the best on his journey. He felt a real sincerity and her generosity as she wished him well, something he wasn't expecting. It was tangible, heartfelt and encouraging. He imagined that Arthur might have inherited his supportive ways from that great lady. Again, he realised what a privileged position he was in, breezing into peoples' lives through his journey and getting to sample what was going on for them in what was their everyday scene. It made him wonder at what it might be like for them having him come into their lives all of a sudden. They continued to chat about the 'old days' in Dingle, and Star Wars, which was being filmed there at the time. He headed off to sleep early again, exhausted.

The next day was Sunday. He and Arthur headed off on foot to Tullamore, where he would leave the Grand Canal. They had good conversation, talking farming; what works and what doesn't, and how they could make a difference through doing what they wanted to do. Arthur was happy that his career landed in his lap and he didn't have to think about it. He seemed to love farming and what he was doing - the freedom of it. He talked about how it was such a good way to raise kids and was very grounding for them to be part of it, growing up. He agreed, remembering his own childhood.

There is hardship in farming, there are good years and bad and the producer is pretty much at the mercy of the markets and the elements. There is a lot of risk involved and this made him think about the world of food he had worked in for many years. Helping grow local food was his work, his career for more than eleven years – he found himself in the world of veg, mainly, and so much of the work he did was driven by environmental ethics and the idea of sustainability. He had worked in buying, selling and developing new markets for local veg, and what he could see, as he walked and talked with Arthur, were his reasons for doing it. Not necessarily because he wanted to save the world, but because of the people. He had worked with small producers because that's what he saw happening around him growing up – small farmers working together, families who had collaborated for generations – community. This was what was important.

In the UK (and likely in Ireland too) he mostly experienced the disconnection of production – a decimated system where buyers had all the power and producers were pitted against each other to lower the price. He wanted to recreate the fairytale world of his childhood with farmers sharing equipment costs and their roles being complimentary rather than competitive. Small-scale production meant a lot to him and all the small producers he worked with cared about biodiversity - about doing something differently in order to both preserve the natural environment and feed people good food.

Resource-based thinking is likely what causes the knocking of ditches to maximise the food production area. In his view, there was already enough food in the world - how people manage the land and transport were the key factors. Knocking ditches to make bigger fields seems like a good idea, but what inadvertently happens is often the wiping out of species through decimating their habitat. The eco system is adapting to pressures put upon it by demand for larger scale farming, but would there be any wildlife left if this goes on unchallenged?

Abandoning peat harvesting, although painful and costing jobs, was likely a good thing as the aim would be to reduce the amount of carbon released into the atmosphere, despite it being difficult to gauge what harm one farmer or grower does by cutting turf or knocking a ditch. His feeling was that community was the way forward. People accepting each other for who they are and supporting each other moving forward, no matter how challenging that may be. It is likely that the world needs a certain amount of large-scale agriculture in the same way it needs small scale. Often, it is difficult to know what the best way forward is.

He talked with Arthur about how he now didn't know what to do next with his life. He had stepped out of a job as a full time, commercial organic veg grower and had worked in that area for the past dozen years. It felt like time for a change. He had left his job and taken a step out into the absolute unknown, spending five months preparing for a journey after which he had no real idea what he would do. Although he was enjoying the journey immensely, he was putting himself under a lot of pressure to come up with 'life solutions' for himself as he went.

Through Water to Road Way

He and Arthur parted ways at Tullamore, which had some picturesque manhole covers. He felt enriched by a couple of days of learning and sharing. He had learned that it was possible to deal with grief without it being a heavy weight - it was more about how people chose to deal with it. He began to see a possibility for himself feeling less sad and weighed down by his troubles and knowing that his life could well take a new direction if that was what he wanted. It was as if this better version of him was just ahead of him on the path, beckoning, giving him a glimpse of who he could be, but at the same time not showing him the route. He had to lose himself, to not know his direction – to trust, as he trusted the many twists and turns in his walk. He was a mass of confusion all the same – a maelstrom of mixed emotions as he left that inspiring time.

The following days he walked alone, stayed with generous, charming people, learned more about the bogs and headed south along the road. He met a generous garage owner in a place called Blue Ball, who loved trucks and drew a route map for him on the back of a 'hot chicken portions' bag. He did an interview for local radio on the phone in a stubbly silage field and felt emotional. He loved how the straight flat of the canal towpath had changed into undulating, unpredictable landscape, the sunny weather bringing a freshness and life into the hedgerows. The quietness of the back roads and the newness round every corner made it feel intriguing and fun. He noticed hills many miles in the distance and guessed which ones he might walk past that day or the next. He was alone and feeling strong, capable and topped up by kindness, support and sharing, seeing that it was OK to talk about sadness and even better to listen.

The Search for Still Waters

He came out of the back roads and into Kilcormac and was immediately bought a coffee by the man who owned the shop there. A few people were standing around and they asked him where he was going, as he was the only person there with a large rucksack on his back. He was interested in the fact that they were hanging out by this shop on a Monday morning. He was told there was a bike race coming through the town and so he decided to wait with them. Again, he felt part of the scene, fitting right in with the gathered crowd. Minutes later the Rás came through; the bikes in a thick bunch, like a flash flood, gears clicking, sounding like some giant insect. The Rás Tailteann is a national, round Ireland cycle race, taking place annually since 1953. Five minutes after that he was on the back road again towards Birr. Had he been five minutes earlier or later he would have missed the whole thing.

He wondered at the causal connections between things, how, even when not planned, interesting and amazing things occurred, the kindness of people could emerge, deep or exciting experiences could happen. He thought about meeting Rita and Anne and how their experiences had been exactly what he needed at that moment. He reflected on how much of his life he felt like he was connected with, how much he just did what seemed to be routine and safe, leaving little room for spontaneity. Those days on the road gave him a strong feeling that if he put himself 'in the way of things' rather than hiding, he might have a different experience of life. He could see that there were both challenges and surprises waiting when he stepped outside 'normal life'. There was a randomness to it that

144

made him feel uncomfortable, yet the pull to experience the unexpected was tantalising.

As he continued, he began to feel the occasional sharp pain in his right foot and felt as if it was going a bit numb. As he lifted his leg with each step, the right toe was beginning to drag on the ground somewhat, and he found he had to lift his right leg a little higher than normal to stop that from happening. This was unexpected and unpleasant, because when he caught that foot on the ground it felt painful. He pretended for a while that it wasn't happening, like he was misjudging his steps, but the truth of injury began to creep into his consciousness and the familiar worry crept in alongside it. Just like being back in Wales he was struggling again with the same questions. "What have I done wrong?" and "What is the pain trying to tell me? Should I be stopping?"

Berating himself for getting it wrong, he once again contemplated failure and how it was likely his fault. He thought of Aoife whose memory helped centre him and helped him to be with the pain and not turn away from it. He reminded himself that in regular life he generally gave up personal goals very easily, like he had a motivation deficit and this was an opportunity for him to keep pushing through, for once. On the walk, life was more physical and practical. He could either finish it or not. He could let the physical stuff stop him or just resolve to keep going - simple choice in this case. He noticed once again how easily he thought about giving up and what a pattern that had always been for him. Almost as if there was a part of him on alert for reasons to give up, to call himself a failure and stick with the old story. Since he knew his thoughts were not who he was, he felt a deeper connection to the idea of moving through the pain, rather than avoiding it. He had kayaked across the Irish Sea, after all!

As he continued, he went between this feeling of worry about the pain and the resolve to stick with it. But the worry was strong and held him. Again he thought about Aoife and felt the pain of their relationship, of how he could not bring himself to truly feel she was the sister he should have had. This too was normally an avoidable pain and he began to see it was one of his oldest habits – to avoid accepting his sister and his grief for her. He felt a deep shame rising within – a wave of feelings about how he had treated Aoife, neglecting her, pushing away thoughts of her and the heaviness and burden he felt every time he went to visit her. He had made it her fault. He had to stop and breathe for a moment to absorb this realisation.

He felt like a bad person; unworthy, incapable, wrong and broken in some way - like Rashkolnikov in Crime and Punishment he had carried within him a dark secret – a denial of love and acceptance for his helpless, innocent sister, now dead. Could he ever repair his relationship with her? It was the most pathetic kind of crime – an unforgivable, inhuman transgression. How could he make it OK?

Then he saw the opportunity to push through that pain too – he realised that he was holding on to his shame, keeping it alive. With that realisation came the feeling of pushing through, an inner knowing that he could release that shame and the bile contained within it that kept him being defensive - hiding his hurt away from people and not letting them get close enough to see it. He had designed his life around this shame and hurt – it was the source of much of his self-doubt, lack of motivation, fear and anger at others and staying small within his life. It was his fear of truly expressing who he was because it might expose him and make him vulnerable, a fear that he might be found out in some way and punished. He could hide no longer.

A Fiver and a Micra

A short time later, on a tree-lined lane he noticed a green Micra pull in off the road just in front of him. He also noticed that there were five adults in the car, which struck him as a little unusual. He felt some kind of intent in this car pulling in and was a little apprehensive as a young man emerged from the rear door and approached him, blurting out "Have you ever thought about where people go after they die?" He stood, superglued to the road for a moment in a kind of startled trance, as this was what he had just been thinking about. What was happening? Where had these people come from? How did they know? The man had a magazine in his hand. It dawned on him that the man was a Jehovah's Witness. He replied that he had thought about death quite a lot, as it happened and had his own ideas and beliefs (that he was still working out). Then the driver got out and asked him if he was the guy who was doing the walk as she'd heard him on local radio. He nodded and smiled a yes. She then motioned to the young man to retreat back to the car. He turned and walked away.

The driver gave him €5, apologised for her brother-in-law and they drove off. He stood there looking at the €5 note in his hand trying to work out what had happened. He looked around and saw a road and fields, some trees on a gently undulating landscape and perhaps no hidden cameras. It was quiet. He asked himself if he wasn't worth saving or if he had passed some kind of spiritual test. He wondered if they were satisfied that he was already on some kind of grief mission. He also wondered where they were heading and whose door they might be knocking on that day and what it took for them to do that. He imagined what the conversation might be in that tiny car as they drove along, the five of them in the Micra. He wondered what happened in the universe for that moment to occur – to meet people on a journey as he was, with all the similarities and differences. His judgement of them as Jehovah's Witnesses, the stigma they had to put up with for their beliefs and 'direct action' style. He walked on, his right foot dragging a little, unless he consciously lifted it higher with each step.

Eco People

That night he had a last minute but very welcome B&B at Cloughjordan Ecovillage, which was a real treat. He was inspired by the people who lived there and their commitment to create a low impact community and all that goes with it. He made the most of his time at the Ecovillage. He was with Joe the baker with whom he had great chats about what was going on at the village, how decisions were being made, who was involved and how things worked. Joe talked about Open Source – making the innovative work one creates free for others to replicate - be it in architecture, farming or energy consumption. There were many parallels between their work and the type of projects he had been involved in over the years in Manchester. He was drawn to the rugged, upbeat, hardy character of the eco-activist.

It was great talking with Joe and neighbour Gregg. They had meaningful conversations about what felt like progress within a system that commodified everything. He felt at home and welcome there. It was another synchronous meeting.

They explored the idea that progress is something that people can construct more quickly together and feed into each other in order to grow and move forward. There seemed like endless opportunities there. He also reflected on the stigma of being part of the 'eco' world and how that too was often frowned upon. People who step out of the relative safety of the middle ground or 'normality' are so often criticised, no matter what they do. He reflected on the irony that the only way humans learn and evolve is through watching and listening to people who step outside the norm.

His foot was swollen and painful that night and he booked in a visit with a local physiotherapist, in the nearby town of Nenagh for the next morning, fearing the worst. He had decided to have a break from walking that day as he wasn't feeling up to it.

There was a carload of them heading to Nenagh from Cloughjordan the next morning and it was good craic on the way in. They went to a cafe as they all had a bit of time to kill before their respective appointments and they chatted about village life, selling vacuum cleaners, what it was like to mix the cob for your own house and the satisfaction of building your own home. He was totally charmed once again by the Ecovillage people and what he regarded as their progressive attitude towards community living, within the wider environment.

He always wondered why people who are vocal about environmental issues are called hippies, etc. This often felt like victimisation on the part of the media, which most likely began in the 1960's in America, when there were mass protests about invasions and war. Hippies and longhairs were victimised and ostracised, beaten and silenced. That is often how mass culture reacts - without understanding or context. It seemed that unless more people actually care about the world they live in, it would be difficult to connect with issues and solve problems as they happen. It's interesting how the media can shape opinion. He felt lucky that he was mainly disconnected from the media and its reporting, growing up with his head in the clouds – he just never thought about any of that. World events didn't occur to him as being important and anyway, he knew he was never getting the whole story.

He knew that, from talking to English friends how the historical relationship between Britain and Ireland was not taught at school in England. His own history lessons were only about oppression and the fight for freedom – in itself an anti-British history. He could see that from interactions with school friends and even from his own behaviour – there was no true story of how the world was. As he followed his heart to work with small producers, people who reminded him of his uncle and the neighbours, he found the alternative, and to him it was a fascinating world. The quiet environmental revolution had to start somewhere, and as more people now embrace protecting the environment.

He wanted to help support small growers, to preserve the practice of being close to the land and not spraying chemicals on everything. His mission was inspired by Dingle, by his feeling of freedom as a boy and the sense that his contribution counted in some way, during harvests and co-operative farm work. Through working with small growers he encountered people with a mission that felt true and real and he didn't need to be interested in global events or know about politics to know that community was well and truly in need of revival.

Where Medical Advice Meets Practical Resolve

The trip to the physio told him he had strained tendons and she recommended he head to the hospital for an x-ray and offered the treatment as a donation. She said that every now and again she gets "weirdos, people like you" in, which made a change from the usual footballers and hurlers she was used to treating.

He then went to the hospital. After the x-ray and analysis he was told he had a stress fracture on a metatarsal bone in his right foot. This, along with the strained tendons meant continuing was not recommended. He had a moment of indecision and overwhelm, thinking he should probably rest, think hard about what to do, maybe even finish the walk early. He would have to quit altogether. A couple of days of rest would not be enough.

He realised that he felt ok and like he could go on. Sure, he was in a bit of pain but he didn't feel awful. He asked each medic "off the record" if someone in his situation was to, hypothetically, sustain those types of injuries, what would be the best way to support those injuries and walk another 120 miles. He got some good hypothetical advice, which was to wrap it up tightly and bathe the foot in ice at the end of each day. He thanked them and went on his way. The hospital also donated the treatment to the walk. He felt supported and strong again. He had happened to keep his walking poles with him and so their time had come.

Sitting in his cousin Susan's house at 4pm after a cup of tea, he felt a moment of commitment and decided to ask her for a lift back to Cloughjordan so he could walk the 'short' ten miles back to her house – his originally planned 'stage' for that day. She kindly agreed, dropping him off in Cloughjordan and he walked the ten miles in just over three hours, feeling strong again – like he had broken through to a new level – going against the 'authority' of the doctors who 'knew better'. But he was beginning to realise that he was the one who knew better – if he trusted himself and didn't just take others' word for it. All his life he had mainly put others' needs and requests first, feeling like *they* always had a better idea of what was going on, as if he did not have the strength to push his own agenda, to show himself courageously in the world. That was the crippling part, more than the injuries he had sustained. This time he was carrying on through, taking the initiative, moving beyond self-pity and uncertainty – the kayaking had showed him that even when he felt like he had nothing left, there was always something in the reserves to tap into. He still had plenty 'in the tank', despite having an injury which, under normal circumstances, would stop him in his tracks.

He left Nenagh, the birthplace of his grandmother, with a feeling of familiarity and as if he'd befriended something whilst there. He walked south and the traffic thundered by. Once again, he'd met family members he was estranged from and felt the bond. It was a gift to be in their company and see the similarities in attitude and insight with his cousin Susan and he wondered whether this was a family trait or just coincidence. Whatever it was it felt gratifying to be opening up to family more – to see how rewarding it was to connect to his own story within the wider family context. Being on a main road again, the loud traffic was unforgiving and harsh, sending him inward.

As a self-proclaimed outsider he was walking home – he was making the biggest statement of love he could, showing his family and the world that he was ready to accept – and to be accepted. He was on his way and wanted to give something back, in terms of the fundraising but also through embracing his home country again – a country he had felt detached from for half his life. Growing up he felt the pain of a people perhaps not yet ready to heal from hundreds of years of oppression, violence and subjugation – the pain of having to hold it in for so long and carry on. His ancestors were repressed through serving the British

Crown by being forced to pay rent on land no longer their own, through not having the freedom to practice their faith, through having to hide their language and culture from a domineering force, committed to exploitation and profit. He began to see that his own reluctance to face the pain of his ancestors, the people who had sacrificed and lived through so much so he could walk freely, was something that had contributed to him hiding his emotions and confidence for most of his life. He needed to feel expressed as a child, but felt that his sensitivity, combined with his culture would not allow it.

His people had struggled and suffered, and that created deep wounds. Wounds for future generations to heal, perhaps. He wanted to acknowledge the hardship borne by those who went before him and so he imagined the lives of his parents' families, of peasant farmers for whom opportunities were so few, being stuck in a cycle of paying rent to a landed Lord. The landlord would have been educated to see the people as a resource, as part of a population to be controlled with a heavy hand, and used for their own elevation within the ruling system. This system, which actively practiced the 'divide and conquer' tactic, whose sole aim was to break up the existing culture and the fabric of community, kept people in fear of them and turned the people against each other wherever possible. It was a supreme act of cruelty and in many ways it was no surprise that growing up in the rural place he did, where this 'apartheid' had been practiced, he felt hopeless and unworthy.

Acknowledgement of this suffering felt important to him – to see that what he felt was not his fault and likely due, in part, to massive cultural shifts and hardships experienced by his ancestors. When his country finally regained self-governance it was a broken culture, having to rebuild itself after the ravages of centuries of discontent. This was the deeper story, which needed to be acknowledged and not just another dark event to leave behind. Ireland, having regained its independence fewer than a hundred years before, was still a young country. The eventual devastating effects of the Civil War and church's involvement in a new Ireland adjusting to independence, ended up compounding the wounds of a people recovering from hundreds of years of oppression - a weakened population putting all its trust in the authority of religious leaders led to many sad and damaging events. Aoife's early treatment, and his own education, in many ways, were part of this dying system, right at its closing stages, when things were thankfully changing for the better, when the ideal of a European culture was in some way attempting to raise everyone up to a new level of unity, perhaps.

But so often he lived in the past, as if England, the country he now called home was still the enemy, in some ways. He felt English people could not fully understand him, nor acknowledge what Ireland had been through. How could they? It was before their time and not even in their education.

Along the hard road he walked, traffic drone the ever-present mantra, the deafening white noise of tyres on tarmac felt aggressive and unwelcoming. He wondered at what people call progress, whilst still being grateful for fast roads. However, the faster people go the less they connect to the land that is moved through. There was an air of indifference about the flow of traffic moving through the countryside and he felt the contrast between their journey and his — theirs seemed like a way between A and B, the road being an obstacle of sorts between two places. His journey sometimes felt that way, but in that moment he connected again with the deeper purpose of his walking — to be able to meet the land with every step, making each one count, and through those steps reconnecting his body with memory, pain, fear, hope and power — whatever came his way. He longed to be free of what previously felt like emotional numbness and cynicism, a feeling that life was not going his way and that people were often not who he thought them to be. He was now recognising that feeling as the heavy weight of a deeper, unacknowledged grief.

The Work of Worry

The days went on in this way — a mixture of enjoyment and uncertainty. He feared finishing the walk. What would he do after that? What would it be like to stop? He wondered about whether or not he was using his time wisely, worrying about what to do next. Anxiety about his life circumstances filled his consciousness — money worries and job worries. His concerns were as long as the road he walked, as long as he chose to tune into it.

Audiobooks were an occasional distraction from the rumination, but it was a big part of his life so he gave it plenty time as he was used to doing. There was a point to the brooding – they were real things he was dwelling on, real concerns and complex situations that needed to be figured out. Or were they? Was his worry perhaps just a way to occupy himself, an escape from what was happening in his life? In a sense, his worry and anxiety were his greatest work – he embraced them with enthusiasm, put time and energy into maintaining and deepening his connection with them – they were his love children, his creative projects. They had been his solid companions and devotees all of his life, his troupe of friends, always there when he needed them. When things got too much, he didn't face those situations and move on, he worried and moved inwards, to hide. He chose worry over action in his life and that was becoming clear. The worry and anxiety felt incongruous with the walk, but as the end was only a few days ahead, those feelings were once again stirred. "What is the purpose of life?" he would ask himself. "What is being a human about?" These worry questions were extremely attractive, inviting existential crisis and reckoning every time. They were the feedback loops of his existence, not really feeling 'of the world' but as if he was an observer there, watching all that went on around him, clever enough to not get involved. He was emotionally unavailable, just standing back and watching from what felt like a safe distance. He realised the extent to which he did this in his everyday life – with his wife, his daughter, with friends and work colleagues – just letting them in enough so he appeared interesting - and aloof enough to be non-committal to friendship or deeper relationship. But there was a price to pay for his non-participation.

His wife, Beth knew him best and put up with his detachment through love, seeing that within him – as within every person – there was someone who wanted to be free of emotional turmoil and feel whole and satisfied. She supported him to leave for a month so he could make steps towards finding that freedom for himself, to make peace with the deep shame he carried within him, that shame which his true self hid behind. His personality began to feel like a façade – a people pleasing automaton whose purpose was to protect a great ball of shame. He had forgotten that behind that shame was where his true self was trapped and had been stuck there for decades, causing a whole host of complexes. He began to see it all and felt scared about what he now knew he had to tackle.

At one point the newly healed blister on his right foot began to feel painful again. It was stinging badly and he knew he had to do something. At his stop that evening, he had to twist the painful right foot round towards him, as far as it could go, then use a mirror reflection (as he couldn't twist it enough to see it) to help him lance the needle blindly through the healed layer of skin. He winced with pain – both from the tendons in the foot he had to twist and when he missed the blister pocket underneath the skin. He eventually struck gold, pus oozing out and he squeezed it out thoroughly – an infection must have occurred through walking on the open, healing blister for many days. Afterwards he fell back on to the floor, gasping and sweating with the effort and pain it took to manage that 'operation.' "Never again!" he told himself, in desperation.

Go South-West, Young Man

He made a commitment to himself to use the journey as inspiration for what was coming next. He could not go back to life as it was, to settle into what he realised was his own stuckness and stagnation. It was lack of movement that kept him where he was. Whatever would come next, he would embrace it. He was ready. Ready to transform, to move, to shed his skin, to leave his shell behind. He stopped to eat a sandwich next to 'De Bucket' pub, sitting on the grass under a young sycamore tree, as it was sunny and quite warm. A man came out and talked to him over the pub wall. His name was Patrick and he'd driven about sixty miles from Banna for some lunch. Patrick was a bit blown away by the fact that he had walked the twelve or so miles from Limerick that day, never mind from Manchester. Patrick insisted on buying him a pint of Guinness, his first of the journey and it was beautiful. He said "I'll be thinking of you, Alan" with such candour that he felt it hit a still place inside, through the self-doubt and mistrust, like Patrick could see that all he needed in that moment was to feel some reassurance.

A Flying Visit

The next day he walked to Foynes, the place where Aoife was 'incarcerated' as a young child. He was feeling confronted by the idea of that place, because as a child he only remembered the heaviness of going there, the grim, spooky building and overworked staff, who always seemed a bit mean – to a five year old anyway. There was sadness to the whole situation, at least he felt sad for little Aoife, locked away in a home seventy miles from his. He had a big block about going there and it felt emotionally taxing just thinking about it. In fact, he was certain it would be a miserable place.

He had yet another room paid for him in Foynes, as a generous donation. He dropped his bag there and went for a walk, wanting immediately to find the hospital Aoife had been in, which he hadn't seen for over thirty years. He asked somebody on the street where the hospital was. They pointed him in the direction of the church. He walked into the car park and saw that next to the church there were some buildings, which were houses for people like Aoife. They were modern buildings and not the place Aoife had been in. He could hear the cries and busyness of the residents inside - a sound that was familiar, which brought up intense feelings and memories.

He walked up to the door, with the idea that he could connect with someone there, find out where the old hospital was and talk a bit about Aoife. He gripped the door handle and thought to himself "I'm not here for this". He let go of the handle, turned and walked back out onto the street. Then, further along he spotted an old, flat roofed building, set on the hill above the main street. He immediately had flashbacks and images of the place where Aoife had been as a little child. He remembered the endless car journeys in the rain, picnics by the side of the road, a sense of excitement and adventure, but also sad, miserable memories, or perhaps more a sense of them, their heaviness.

Below that building, on street level was a museum and the back end of what looked like a plane was sticking out beside it. He was shocked and was compelled to walk into this museum because he was so surprised to see it, just here next to 'Aoife's prison'. It was called 'The Flying Boat Museum'. There was a lady in the ticket office. In the 1940's the first transatlantic flights went from Foynes. The building looming behind, which looked like some kind of boarded up, Eastern Bloc prison was in fact an art deco hotel, built to accommodate those who alighted from the Boeing B314 Flying Boat and needed somewhere to rest overnight. These transatlantic passenger flights all took place in the 1930's and 40's.

So the hospital was built as an ultra-modern hotel! The Pan Am Clipper flying boat had brought such people as JFK, and Humphrey Bogart to Foynes and, as he floated round this museum on a cloud of almost disbelief that this even existed, it started to colour the dim perspective he'd had of Foynes. The museum also consisted of a big chunk of plane, which he looked around and sat in. He tried to imagine what it might be like to bounce around the sky in the belly of this noisy, prop-engined beast before dropping on to a watery runway and mooring up. What an experience that must have been!

The Flying Boat Museum lady told him that, when she was a child that building was where the doctor and the dentist were located too. "When we went to the dentist we could hear the children crying above" she grimaced. It didn't sound too pleasant. To him, as a child, the building felt scary and the people were scary and he hadn't wanted to be there. It reminded him of the Victorian building he'd had his first years of school in and which felt like it had Victorian values of strictness and discipline. Were those feelings related to how he felt about the hospital in Foynes? Was there some link between this and Ireland's ailing, pious, rural education system, which had put 'the fear' into him.

Being there that day, however, was cathartic. He saw how there was nothing bad or wrong about the place itself. He still had the irrational, impressionable memories of a little boy guiding him. It made him think about the complexity of experiences that go into making a person who they are, and the influence those experiences have on beliefs and decisions. People are often led blindly by emotions, which can be based on decisions made as very young children, with little or no emotional intelligence. His own complexes were proof of that.

He knew that visit was of great importance for him, illuminating the difference between decisions he had made as a child and the reality of what he saw, thirty-five years later. There was no truth to a situation, he was sure of that. The truth of his own memory was not a fixed thing and could be changed. The fact that he had avoided Foynes all his life made him feel a bit silly. A bit like learning to swim. It was actually easy to face.

Allowing Support

The following day he walked across the border to his home county, Kerry, which felt strange. Only four days' walking remained ahead of him to figure out the rest of his life. He stopped that evening at Mag and Tom's, more friends of friends he had never met before. They hit it off straight away. Mag talked about being in the bog. She said she'd been in the bog all day and what a great place it was to be. He wasn't sure what she meant at first but then he realised her connection with the land was deep. He was hooked in, hanging on her every word. She grew her own veg and appeared truly satisfied with the life she had and her surroundings. They talked about growing organic food and met eye to eye on so many levels. He felt deeply satisfied in her presence. After the hard couple of days and confusing emotions it was a joy to be at Mag and Tom's house. She was a welcoming and accommodating soul, into the power of plants and nature, connecting with her surroundings, learning from the land. He had an ice footbath and then relaxed on the bed. They had a lovely dinner and met her husband Tom who was quiet and seemed wise. He struggled to understand what Tom, whose local accent was strong, was saying at times. He reflected that he had been away for so long he didn't understand his own people any more. What did that mean for him? Tom went out again and they talked about Aoife and the family. Mag reassured him he was following his need as a brother to look after and protect Aoife – and he could not be blamed for feeling helpless and powerless in that situation, as a child. He began to feel a soothing wave wash over him. He needed peace and to know that he had done all he could as a brother to his little sister. He needed that reassurance and felt it like a warm embrace to his lonely soul.

Into Stillness

It was a beautiful, cloudless evening and they sat in the living room watching the sun slowly set. He had been out all day and was happy to watch it from the inside. The weather couldn't have been more perfect. It seemed to calm everyone and felt just right. Mag was preparing him a seaweed footbath, as Tom returned to the house. He felt a little embarrassed as the kind of people he had grown up around would definitely never have a seaweed footbath, nor would they be giving one to guests. It felt luxurious to be cared for in that way. He then got talking to Tom again and somehow began to understand him. Perhaps they both relaxed a bit and were then able to communicate more clearly. Mag handed him a hot whiskey to go with the footbath and he sank into a luxurious place of peace. His state of relaxation was reaching a new level, one that had perhaps never before been reached. He felt their open generosity and welcome and yet he still found it hard to receive. He didn't want to put them out and perhaps he felt that he didn't deserve to be treated so well. They all chatted about foraging and seaweed and there was a great connection between them – it was more than words. He could feel it. It was the feeling of his people, those who lived simply and worked on the land, communing with the landscape. He could identify with this and it reminded him of his Uncle Tom and of the simple beauty his childhood held. In that moment he felt privileged to have experienced some kind of connection to a fleeting truth of existence, with the past and future all as one. He realised what really mattered is feeling at home in one's surroundings, being settled and satisfied and able to interact with as much of it as possible. There was love in the room and he could feel it healing his lonely heart, as if their groundedness was holding him, showing him that all was ok, that all he had to do was relax and let go. The moment was so satisfying that he experienced a kind of reverie, as if he were leaving his body and returning to feel the warmth of what he could only describe as healing energy. He was amazed at the power of people and how they could share a moment together - to be vulnerable, to heal and to intuit a response to a situation.

Writers Walk

Walking into Listowel the next day there was a sign for Listowel Writers' Week and he felt pride as he was reminded of the writer John B Keane, who wrote plays about rural Irish life. He remembered 'Sive', which he studied at school. A tragic play set in the 1950's about an arranged marriage for money between an old farmer and a beautiful young woman. The old man had little to say to her when they first met besides "I have the intention of buying a motoring car, and by all means women do be driving them too." A line that always stuck with him. "Everyone knows walking is better", he thought to himself.

He was a few days early for the festival but it was exciting to be there and also he loved the idea that a town like Listowel, which as a child he knew mainly as the place where the milk from his Uncle's cows went to be processed, had produced a legendary writer like Keane, and a literary tradition of its own. Again, he felt proud of his home county and was looking forward to a pint in John B's famous pub. That afternoon he wistfully wrote in a café with floral tablecloths, looking out the window of the café at the sunny, busy street, reflecting on Aoife again. He enjoyed writing in the busy café and for a moment felt light and carefree. He was nearly home.

The following day, after a night of a few pints with an old school friend and some much needed abandon and laughs with the locals at John B's Pub, he hit the road to Tralee. He was meeting people from home now, his Uncle Jim was the first of the day. Trucks and cars were flying by and he was again feeling a bit shaken up by the traffic. It was relentless. Jim wanted to take him to a café somewhere but he was keen to stay on the road so they talked in the car for 20 minutes about endurance and walking. Jim told him how he'd injured himself preparing for a marathon once and couldn't run it. His uncle said he looked strong despite the fracture. Jim was going to Lough Derg, to a retreat for 3 weeks. After saying goodbye he wondered what he would be doing on retreat and what his uncle's idea of enlightenment was.

He walked on and an hour later met Seán, a news reporter and old school friend. They did some filming and Seán left. A few miles on, he met another Dingle man, who had randomly come to bring him water and walk a little with him. He and Gene walked and talked for a bit and Gene showed him how to hold his walking poles correctly. He had been walking with them held incorrectly for a week at that point. Gene's presence was comforting and light. It was cheering to feel that he was getting closer to home and people were actually coming to see him.

Once Gene left, he began to imagine what it would be like to get home. There was a plan to meet a bunch of people at the top of the Conor pass – one of Ireland's highest road passes at around 450m, which sweeps down to sea level on each side and on a clear day is a great way to experience the breadth and dramatic scenery of the Dingle peninsula. Walking along with still about 8 miles to go 'till Tralee, he felt the heat bouncing off the tarmac. He imagined meeting his family. The sense of achievement and vulnerability he was feeling at making such a journey for himself and his family, in so many ways, brought a lump to his throat. His eyes filled with tears for the journey nearing its end, for his life and its sadness, for his sister and for his family. He shed tears and felt the accomplishment of what he had done. He savoured that moment of connection to achievement, anticipating little 'solo' time from then on. The road became curvier and he began to catch a glimpse of the Kerry mountains, those he could see from his window, growing up, but from a different angle. He had reached Tralee, the town he was born in. Only 30 miles to go.

Happy Daze

Having been out in the sun all day he reached Colin's house, another friend of a friend. They hit it off well, having had similar life experiences. It felt almost surreal as he talked with Colin and his housemate about rewilding and conservation and how it was to look at the world in an ecological way. Once again a kind of synchronicity was occurring, an experiment to find out who he resonated with the most. He had the feeling of connection, peace and support and he bathed in its soft energy, and went to bed that night wishing to hold on to that fleeting feeling.

He wondered what the difference was between those he connected with and those he didn't. Why was he open to some and not others – often only open to those he considered to be 'doing the right thing' or being the sort of person whose actions he approved of. This was a question that had kept him on the periphery for a long time, not wanting to commit to a certain ethos or belief system – because he wanted to know what the difference was between someone who worked in conservation and say, a ruthless capitalist, who he didn't want to listen to.

All his life he had put others' opinions before his own, listened to others' rants and being right about things, never really knowing his own opinions, within the confusion of everyone else's. He knew that his character was gentle and perhaps that was what drew him to what he was interested in – not chasing the money or career but looking at what he considered important – taking care of the land and the people who worked it, who earned very little money and did what he considered to be a very important job. He could easily dismiss a petrochemical engineer or someone who worked selling derivatives as people doing evil to the world. He wondered where this opinion came from, where those judgements came from and whether they interfered with his own satisfaction of life. He always knew, growing up that each person – even those who he didn't like and who had hurt him – had their own reasons for being who and how they were. What he didn't do was count his own opinion as important within it all. He was beginning to realise that in some ways it was OK to accept the bully's way of being as well as the gentle person's – but as equals, not as different from each other.

What he rejected about the capitalist or the Jehovah's Witness in training was only what he didn't understand, and by taking comfort and agreeing with only the familiar he realised he was closing himself off to others and to possibilities of growth. Where did his scale of judgement of 'right and wrong' come from? How could he chastise people for flying around the world or starting a business that pays a very low wage to people in developing countries? He realised that without knowing the whole story there was no way he could make a judgement on others and what impact they made on the world. Could he *ever* know the whole story? He began to see the world as a continuously changing landscape and just as he was walking and moving through places and interactions, the world was also moving through cycles and changes, stages of development and not working toward some ultimate goal. There seemed to be so much tension in the world and very little acceptance, just as there was within him.

He had begun his journey of acceptance of the parts of him he pushed away, the grief and pain he had all his life felt ashamed of. Was he also doing the same thing by walking away from people he didn't agree with or dismissing the clerk in the derelict hotel in Wales who told him he was off his head for walking from Manchester? What were these interactions telling him? That he might only be happy once he had considered accepting all parts of himself and not just the ones he felt others approved of? That he need not judge or see separation between himself and others? That everyone is just trying their best? That this life is complex and ever-changing and what he didn't understand he generally tended to view negatively in some way. As early humans learned to mistrust the approaching animal, he was now willing to let go of an ancient fear of the unknown. The peace he was feeling was important, but it wasn't the answer. He got a sense that for him an answer might lie in going deeper into his own experience of life, therefore freeing himself from his long held pain and sadness. He wanted to connect with people and move outside his comfort zone in order to do that. He'd had a glimpse of what was possible, in that moment.

Last Legs

The following days were the end of the walk. He met his father and sister in Tralee, did a radio interview and walked the road home from Tralee, together with his sister Susan - on a very familiar road. The weather was again sunny and warm. He and Susan chatted and made their way to Castlegregory, where they were to stay at another kind lady's generosity. There he had his first swim in the tepid-feeling seawater. Castlegregory's soporific sandy roads brought a soft-focus feel to the place. It was like a seaside resort in Sri Lanka he'd been to a few years before or like walking barefoot to the beach with his mother and sister when he was a child, where soil became sand, oozing out of the roadside verge. He wanted to cocoon there, to go into stasis with Beth and Rae, who had arrived after the long drive from Manchester. This would do. Long beaches to walk the dog and dramatic landscapes. He could learn to surf, maybe even open up a surf shop as Dee had surprised him by suggesting, in Dublin. In truth, he had no idea what would happen next. There was no permanent job to go back to, no money to speak of, just the willingness to finish the journey and see what happened.

The next day he and his sister, Susan walked the last miles uphill towards Pedlar's Lake they met Seán the journalist again, who filmed the ascent towards the Conor Pass, An Chonair, as it was known 'as Gaeilge.' He knew there would be a crowd waiting and felt nervous and withdrawn but grateful once he saw everyone there. They all walked the last four miles downhill into town together where his family had arranged a spread for him. He chatted but felt quiet inside. When they were getting in the car to go home he asked his parents to take his daughter so he and Beth could walk the last couple of miles together, as they had walked the first few. Heading out the road he had walked a thousand times, with the harbour and Burnham tower on the right, past Fungie the dolphin's playground, was easily the best part of the walk – that familiar way, Beth next to him, without hurry or stress, nor care of pain or injury. They walked together, excited to be reunited and for the time they would have together in the days that followed. He felt very grateful for that amazing woman, who had fully supported him to make the journey possible, who stood by him for years, patiently observing his quiet suffering and stuckness and also willingness to feel free. There was no doubt then, no thought of tomorrow or of the past, no feeling of loss or physical pain. Only a couple of people, chatting and laughing, walking out the main road home on a warm, still summer evening, the day after their nine year wedding anniversary.

The End - Summer 2021

We are nature. Every living thing is nature and I feel we are taken away from our connection to this through busyness and multiple distractions. 2020 was an eye opener for me. I was extremely busy in the world of local food all the way through lockdown number one and experienced furlough during lockdown two. There have been many different experiences of this pandemic. Many have suffered and continue to suffer extreme hardship. Some have had an incredibly busy time of it through 2020 and 2021, having to work and serve people in some way. People have experienced hardship at the 'front lines' of this epidemic, but from my own, small experience of this I can say that one thing I learned through this force of nature, is to be more accepting of what is happening for others, to be in that space of learning when it comes to what people were struggling with, even if I feel like disagreeing with their behaviour on some level. One person wishes to be away from other people because they don't feel safe, another person thinks it's all a scam and a conspiracy and they don't feel safe. Some people felt controlled and others felt like isolation was the only sensible thing to do. I learnt that whatever makes people feel safe to express their feelings about the situation, without bringing harm to themselves or anyone else, is fine. Sometimes I think we spend a lot of our lives trying, in whatever way we can, to make ourselves feel safe.

There is a stimulus within all of this. Through being locked down, many people, lucky enough to have some green areas nearby, could experience nature in a new way. I have talked to people about how they have recently been observing the same scene they had been seeing for years, in different ways, as if those scenes had come to life for them once they had no choice but to tune in. In having to stay in one place for an extended time, what they found was the power of being still. This seems to tune people into what is important to them – family, those close to them, place and the power of slowing down.

I don't personally know anyone who died from the virus, but I know people who got very ill and some who remain ill, even a year later. There is no doubt the virus affects us in many ways - bringing up fear, resistance, grief and many other emotions we may have kept a lid on for a long time, under the surface.

I like to sleep out in the hills near my house. I do it regularly as it both grounds me and connects me with the natural world and my own life. When the craziness of the first wave of the pandemic struck in Spring 2020, the world felt like it was collapsing in on itself, there was panic and we were feeling the crush of everything closing down. I walked out into the dark of the night to a nearby familiar spot, within a copse of young birch trees and bedded down to the sound of the stream. Then I noticed it. The stillness. In that moment, nature was still. My mind kept flipping between the chaos that was work and the feeling of the 'end of times,' and then back to the quiet that was around and beneath me, just the gentle roll of water over stone to be heard. I wondered how the world, the actual land was taking the pandemic. It seemed to be fine with it and that helped me to not panic, showed me I had a choice to either be still or go with the wave.

On my long journey I learned that through pushing away emotional memories and experiences I had made life very difficult for myself — and that it wasn't my fault that I did this. I hadn't learned to be with the circumstances I found myself in. I never accepted my sister or really got to know her and that's something I'm learning to be OK with. We all suffer and struggle, with apparently no time to heal ourselves and feel a bit more connected. Then the pandemic came along and showed us many things — that life can change forever in a moment, and that we are ultimately not in control of what happens to us, as much as we might want to feel like we are.

The Way it Was

We are waiting for when the world 'returns to normal', but nature does not allow things to be as they were before. We have an opportunity to let that go and embrace the new with what we have learned through this global lockdown. Whether we judge it to be bad or good, we are not going back to how things were. We only move on, as ever, into uncertainty.

We are being called to change, for our own lives and for the lives of others, for the world that needs our attention and love. We can guide ourselves through our experience of life, not controlling but being with this blend of our nature and our otherness — consciousness, spirit, soul, energy — call it what you want. I believe it is possible to bring these forces together in order to feel satisfaction, connection and peace, in life.

Nature is ever-changing and we cannot control it, just like we cannot control what happens to our bodies as they age, and how we don't know what will happen tomorrow. This is nature. We cannot fix the world. We want to fix ourselves, our broken minds, our grief-filled hearts and world-weary bodies. We can only open ourselves up and allow nature in – the land, people and experiences. It is not for fixing, because there is no fix for what we're experiencing.

Our latest vision for climate change seems to be saying 'It's not too late,' and I like that, because I believe it never is too late. 'It's not too late' gives hope, and it might help us stop long enough to start to look at ourselves, too. 'It's not too late' is like the question, 'if you were on your deathbed, what would you regret not doing?' I feel lucky enough to have asked myself that question, and continue to do so. It helps me to look at myself, make some moves, shake myself up, feel and start to heal the pain that needs my attention. It's not too late.

There is Only Acceptance

There is only being with our situation. We want to fix it all – just as I did during my walk - I desperately wanted to fix myself or be fixed. Instead, all I was doing was pushing away my experience of what my life was. I didn't accept my sister's condition, I didn't accept my feelings towards her, I didn't accept my past. For the most part, I did not accept what I was going through –

the pain, the emotional turmoil – all of it got the better of me for most of the journey. I didn't accept myself as a worthy person, making a contribution, and I did not accept my experience of life as worthwhile or how I wanted it to be. I had always thought it should be different, that *I* should be different. This attitude, I now see everywhere: we want to change the world, to fix it. We want to fight the virus, we say we'll beat it. More than anything, we want to change the world so we don't feel bad about what we're doing to it. We want to change what's happening 'out there,' so we can feel better 'in here', within ourselves. It doesn't work that way. Culturally, we are running away from pain. We are lost in feeling bad, stuck focusing on the problems.

What I learned from my walk is that change first takes place within, not out there, in the world. We have the opportunity to take care of ourselves and each other first. This means actually managing our stress, which makes us avoid and forget who we are, and maintaining connection with family or friends, place and what it is to be human. We share a consciousness with every living thing, the ability to connect to maintain relationships. It is all nature. Connection is what matters, whether that's connection with the world around us or with our own sense of inner peace – this is what matters. Life is only short. We can take opportunities as they arise, be open to adventure and the unknown, and the benefits they bring. It's not an easy thing to do, but the rewards are big.

I spent decades running away, losing myself in the 'work hard, play hard' ethic, as worker and activist, burning out and blaming everyone for what was wrong.

The Search for Still Waters

I was running away from the boy who couldn't express himself, the decisions that boy had made in order to feel safe and the consequences those decisions had brought. I needed to become OK with all that to start living and feeling free, instead of being stressed and losing myself in work and boozing, which I saw as more important than my own sense of satisfaction and happiness. The irony is not lost on me. I know that without those experiences I would not have the perspective I gained. So, in some way, was it all meant to be? Was it what I needed to eventually come to this point? A perfectly imperfect story, ready for me to choose how to feel about it.

That walk opened up a path of healing for me, an adventure, that my four hundred mile walk and paddle was just the beginning of. I continued on. For me it took courage to take that path of healing with conviction and confidence. I had to keep going within and face fears. I had to get to a place where I wasn't dogged by depression any more. This book is my testament to that search for answers, and that journey, which really was one man's search for meaning – to connect with the story of my life and face the things that stopped me, the attitudes that drew a veil of cynicism over my vision of life. The words were often difficult to write and to feel OK about. I had to dig deep and work through the pain, to actually see it through. There was no more avoiding it. Sometimes it just felt like too much, too close, which is why I chose to write it in third person, for the most part.

Since that journey I've had five years of change, of pain and joy, some suffering and lots of acceptance, of questioning and learning, and woven into that journey was writing this book. And that change will continue. My children bring me that sense of acceptance and change every day. I've finally settled down to accepting and knowing I can't control, I can only allow and participate, and so it will continue, this perfectly imperfect journey.

The Search for Still Waters

Aoife

And finally, introducing my sister Aoife. In a way I never knew her, in the words of her carer family, beautiful words that make me both sad and happy:

Dear Alan,

I don't know if you remember me, but I met you in Dingle with Aoife on one of our days out. Aoife and I met you and we went out to see Fungie on the boat, and had lunch afterwards. My name is Audrey Bainton and I worked in St. Austin's with Aoife for many years. We were great friends, and I 'befriended' her with the help of your Mother, Social Worker and the Unit Head at the time. This allowed me to bring her outside of campus, to give her opportunities that at the time were very hard to achieve at St Mary's. Back in those days, St. Marys only had one bus and each unit on campus, only had the bus once a month. So outings were very slim. Now thankfully each house has their own vehicle.

Aoife, Aoife, Aoife...where do I start....she was a character. She knew what she wanted and she knew what she liked. There were other characters in St. Austin's with her too, of course and they all enjoyed each other's company and their different personalities. I suppose because the unit was small, they all grew up together sharing the same spaces and things every day. If something happened to any one of them, they all felt it and worried about each other too. They laughed at each other's antics and talked to each other {in their own way}. An example of this was when a room on the unit became available. It had been an office, which was being relocated. We all thought this was a great opportunity for Aoife to have her own room, as she loved going to bed and having her own space in the evenings. She got her own CD player and CDs, massage oils and foot spa. She got a comfy armchair in the corner, to sit in and relax. We painted and decorated it for her and thought she would love it!!! Boy were we wrong...she didn't like it at all, being away from the others, she didn't sleep as well and preferred to go back with the gang. They were that close. She liked the room to get away for a while during the day. She loved having her hands and feet massaged. She loved listening to her music...But that was it! She didn't want to sleep there. She used the room for her own advantage! In the new unit she shared a lovely big room with one other friend - she liked the company.

On the unit at that time the radio was always on with the latest chart music. Aoife, when relaxing liked classical music very much. But she liked dance and disco music too. We are talking about the 1990's onwards!!!! I remember some of the songs were 'Blue (da ba dee)', Sex on the Beach by T-Spoon, Cotton Eye Joe and Sweat by Inner Circle were some of the hits that got her head bobbing!!! She laughed if anyone of us were singing along or dancing and would bop her head along too. She would also roll her tongue and sing along in her own way, with a fit of laughing too. Of course she loved listening to anything anyone got up to at the weekend and loved to be in the middle of the craic. If she didn't approve, she could roll those eyes at you with disgust!!!

The Search for Still Waters

Aoife loved swimming. As you probably know it was a heated pool on the grounds of St. Mary's, so it was delightful to be in at any time. She loved the freedom in the water and loved to float in it for as long as possible. While holding her under her back she loved to be glided through the water, around and around and from side to side. She loved the warm water lapping up onto her.

Same when out for a walk, the faster you went, the more she enjoyed it. She loved being active and out and about. Even if it was doing jobs on the unit, once she was with you, and included in the activity, watching you fold clothes or organising for supper, whatever, once she was occupied she was happy. Of course in the evenings, she loved to be the first to bed. Once she hit the mattress she'd get a fit of laughing!!! It really was her favourite spot.

Horse riding was one of the activities I used to do with her. She liked it and had good balance on the horse too. If you think about it, she was very brave to sit on the horse in the first place. It wasn't a natural sitting position for her. But she did it, and she liked the freedom of sitting on it and the movement of the horse under her too. She wasn't afraid to have a go and give it a try.

I brought her to see the local pantomime a few times. She loved the music, singing and dancing. She was well known backstage and always met the cast afterwards. Of course she'd have a cuppa while there too. She was quite the celeb! Sometimes if the show was going on for too long, she could get tired and start humming...that meant she wanted to go. She was funny with the humming; there were different tones to her humming and different rhythms. It's hard to explain, but you knew the happy, content one and you definitely knew the cross one!!! She was just like you and me, I'm sure people close to you know your tone too!

When I got married in 2002, Aoife was there for the big day. She looked lovely and enjoyed the day and she stayed well into the evening. She enjoyed a glass of wine, you know. The staff that accompanied her were great to bring her and stay until she was ready to leave. I was thrilled she was there with me, but she did give me that look! I don't think she thought much of the Tiara on my head!!!

Aoife was a pleasure to get to know. She had a great personality with a devious laugh, but only showed it if she felt comfortable with you. She was quite prim and proper.... Some thought she had an air about her. But she was just quiet, and only spoke when she had something to say. She was that kind of a person, independent and strong. She was happy in herself. She was caring and gentle and a good listener. She was a good friend, and is missed every day.

Audrey Bainton

****
****

I had the pleasure to meet Aoife in Sept 2000 when I began working in St. Austin's Unit, which is where she lived. It was a big change to work with people who were totally dependent on us for every need.

The Search for Still Waters

Aoife was not going home for Christmas that year. At the start we were all very disappointed for her but as time went on it became easier to understand as we realised the level of care that Aoife needed every day and night.

I enjoyed Aoife's personality as she seemed so aloof at times. She had a way of looking down; she was often confused for a Duchess. It was lovely knowing Aoife and getting to know her. She had a great social life; we went to see Westlife and Shane Ward in concert in Killarney. She could enjoy a glass of wine on occasion.

One of the nicest things I witnessed was the visits from her mom and aunt. Between the two of them, they would rub Aoife's hair for ages, which I really think she absolutely loved. She would be as content as can be, like a cat purring, really.

Sometimes we would get Aoife out of her wheelchair and sit with her on the couch, careful that she wouldn't slip off. Aoife could suffer from very painful ear infections, which would upset her a lot.

She frequently attended the pantomime in Killorglin with one of us and Audrey. When we introduced personal outcomes and keyworker systems, Gemma became her keyworker. This meant that Aoife had her own special person who became her voice and together with her family were able to make plans and goals like visits home, which I think became very special for everyone. Sadly Aoife passed away in 2011 and we really missed her. I have good memories of Aoife and when I am ever in St. Austins, I still see it as her bedroom.

It was poignant when Aoife passed that she spent her last night at home. She had come the full circle.

Marie

****

I first began working with Aoife in March 2000 in St. Austin's unit. When I began working in St. Austin's they had just moved from the main house to this beautiful new building on campus a few days previously so it was a big change for everyone. But everyone settled in well. I will always remember my first day meeting her, as if I wasn't nervous enough starting in a new unit, I remember walking in and being introduced to Aoife and the other residents. She glanced at me out of the corner of her eye, stuck out her tongue and gave a sigh, turning her head the other way. I remember thinking "Oh she won't like me at all" but it did not take me long to get to know her and for her to get to know me. I soon realised that it was all a front and underneath was a gentle, soft, beautiful lady. Aoife was truly a pleasure to care for and get to know.

Aoife came across very aloof, but this was her way. She had to get to know you first before she felt comfortable enough to show her true self. Aoife was a lady of leisure; she enjoyed the finer things in life like the odd glass of wine and of course listening to her classical music. I have no doubt in another life she was a lady of grandeur.

Aoife also loved her own space; she liked to spend time in her own company but she liked to have people around her too.

I went on to become Aoife's key worker up until the time of her passing in 2011. During this time I got to know Aoife quite well and also got to know your family and it really was a pleasure. Aoife loved having visits from the family. When your mother and your Aunt Margaret came to visit her, she would be in her element with one sitting at each side of her both stroking her hands and rubbing her face. She really was in heaven. She loved having their undivided attention.

In later years Aoife began having visits home for an hour or so. Aoife appeared to enjoy these trips, we usually went on to have lunch or supper or a snack out as well and she also enjoyed this. Aoife enjoyed receiving cards and letters in the post from the family and always listened intently when these were read out to her by the staff.

Over the years I accompanied Aoife on several different outings and daytrips. The ones that stand out to me were going to see Westlife play in Killarney, going to watch Ireland play in the world cup on the big screen in the INEC and a day out we had in Muckross farm. She liked being out and about but she also loved arriving back knowing she would get a rest in her chair.

Aoife loved her comfort, whether it was in her comfort chair, on her bed or on the beanbag, she loved to stretch out. For the first few years she shared her bedroom with another resident but she had her own room for the last few years of her life. It took her a while to get used to sleeping on her own but she came to love her tranquil space. Her room was lovely with nice personal pictures around her bed. She loved going to bed and she would just smile and her whole body would visibly relax once she was in bed. She always like to listen to her music for a while when she went to bed. I remember one year, you sent in a copy of the CD you made. She always enjoyed when we put it on for her, it wasn't her usual genre of music but she was always relaxed and content when it was played.

She also enjoyed nothing more than stretching out on her heated waterbed, watching all the sensory lights floating around the room and ceiling in the sensory room. She enjoyed a lot of activities on the unit, like getting her nails painted, having massages and reflexology and footspas. She really loved her jacuzzi baths, going to the pool on campus and going for walks.

She loved touch, especially light touch and loved nothing more than someone running their fingers through her hair, when you stopped she would give a sigh and you would know she wanted you to continue. She really enjoyed her massages but she was very ticklish. I remember trying to give her a foot massage one day and she just could not contain the laughing each time I touched her feet. We had to give up. She had the most beautiful soft skin, especially on her hands.

Aoife communicated through non-verbal communication and facial expression and noises. She had a thing she would do with her tongue and you always knew she was content and happy, when you heard that sound. Her humming was very distinct around the home, you also knew from the humming when she was happy and content and you would always know when she was not happy, the humming would get louder and faster, if there was something that she was not happy about she would have no problem letting you know. I remember if there was a time she was really annoyed she would clench her fists and bring both her arms and legs into her body. I remember this happening on an occasion when Daniel o Donnell was on a DVD in the dayroom. Needless to say we had to take Aoife to another room.

Aoife liked to have your full attention during meal time. If she felt you were talking too much during meals she would give one of her sighs and give you her famous look out of the corner of her eye and of course she was right! She really enjoyed her food. She had a really sweet tooth and would savour every last bit of taste in her mouth.

Aoife was a quiet, content lady, who liked what she liked; she was her own person and knew what she wanted.

Since Aoife's passing a lot has changed in St. Austin's, many of the residents who lived with Aoife have also passed away since, may they all rest in peace. They were a really lovely bunch to work with and I have very fond memories of working there, it was truly a pleasure to go into work each morning.

Gemma

About the Author

Alan worked for many years in the vibrant sustainable, local food sector in Manchester and loved it, gaining a wealth of knowledge and experience in food activism and working with some great people. But he knew he wanted more. In 2016, Alan made a decision to change his life. Through making that journey (involving a 600km hike and 100km sea kayak) he began to view life differently and in a more empowered way. It was about taking control – and also – letting go control. He began training with Way of Nature UK which took him on a journey inwards, connecting him to nature through 24 and 72 hour solo vision quests in wild surroundings, as well as other deepening practices.

Alan and his family moved to Italy in early 2017 for more adventures and, 18 months later returned to the UK to live in the West Yorkshire hills where he works part time in local food, writes, teaches meditation, walks and lives with his family.

Alan likes to think that we can do it ourselves and with a little guidance it is possible for anyone to have a deeper experience of life, learn to guide themselves and stay open to beauty and the simple things in life. Through writing his blog and shadow integration work, Alan is always evolving his passion for communication, self-exploration and holding space for others. He has been doing mindfulness training with the Mindfulness Association for the past couple of years and now teaches the excellent 8 week Mindfulness Based Living Course. He has developed a passion for liberating the mind from oppressive thoughts and mind states and ideas through this brain training practice and will work on combining this with the naturally liberating elements of nature connection work in the coming years. He regularly sleeps out in the hills in a bivvy bag, enjoying the connection and solace that brings, open to whatever comes.

Alan has played drums in bands for many years and enjoys getting involved in music projects.

Find Alan Creedon on the following platforms:

www.endless-river.org
and
https://www.instagram.com/alan_creedon_/